DISCOVERING

WHO

I AM

DISCOVERING

WHO I AM

FINDING YOURSELF IN THIS WORLD,

WHEN YOU'RE NOT OF THIS WORLD

ASHLEY FRIEDRICHS

DISCOVERING WHO I AM

Finding Yourself in This World, When You're Not of This World

ASHLEY FRIEDRICHS

First Edition

ISBN-13: 979-8-9929258-0-7

Imprint: Independently Published

Cover design by Benj Mori

DEDICATION

To my incredible parents, Alex and Len Friedrichs. Your unwavering love and support have made this journey possible. If I could choose my parents a thousand times over, I would always choose you.

ENDORSEMENTS

"In this powerful book, Ashley Friedrichs offers a raw and transparent look into her journey, sharing the deep revelations that God has placed in her heart. Through her authenticity and vulnerability, she invites readers to embrace their own divine calling, no matter where they are in life. The words within these pages not only inspire but also equip and transform, helping you unlock the God-given potential inside of you. No matter what season you're in, this book will guide you toward stepping into God's best for your life —empowering you to live with purpose and faith."

Perla Kent
One College Pastor

We live in a world full of noise and information. All around us we hear voices telling us who we should be, how we should act, and how we do not measure up. How refreshing it is to find content that is focused on combating the lies. In the pages of this book you will find vulnerability as Ashley candidly shares the challenges she faced, the lies she believed, and the problems that created. You will also find your biggest cheerleader reminding you of who you really are and what a spectacular gift you are to the world when you are brave enough to live authentically you!

This is the book we all wish we would have had as we entered college or made our way into adulthood. I highly encourage you to make this your go-to graduation gift for the young adults you love and cherish.

Misty Westlund
Wife & Mom, International Speaker,
Minister, Life Coach/Biblical Counselor

TABLE OF CONTENTS

ACKNOWLEDGEMENTS

First and foremost, thank You to God—none of this would be possible without Him. Thank you to my amazing family, Tara Brown, Pastor Perla, and Hailey Morgan for believing in me, praying for me, and supporting me in every way throughout this process. A special thank you to Krista Dunk and Catherine Timmons for helping me bring the vision God gave me to fruition.

FOREWORD

In a world where young adults are constantly bombarded with messages telling them who they should be, how refreshing it is to come across a book like "Discovering Who I Am." This young author's raw and transparent account of her own struggles and journey towards finding her identity in God is a beacon of hope in a sea of confusion.

As I delved into the pages of this book, I was struck by the author's vulnerability and honesty in sharing her innermost thoughts and experiences. Through her words, she offers practical steps for self-discovery while also providing a sense of camaraderie for those who may feel lost or alone in their own identity crises.

This book is a testament to the power of authenticity and faith in guiding us towards a deeper understanding of who we are meant to be. It is my hope that as you read these words, you will find solace in knowing that you are not alone in your journey and that there is always hope for finding others whom you can relate to.

May this book be a source of encouragement and inspiration for all who seek to discover their true selves in the midst of life's challenges. Embrace the journey, for in it lies the key to unlocking the beautiful masterpiece that is you.

With Abundant Hope,
Ruby Lay
Founder of Hope91 Ministry,
Ordained Minister, Certified Life Coach

CHAPTER 1

UNMASKED

My hair was perfectly curled, and I had just finished applying my makeup. As I sprayed my setting spray and evaluated my reflection in the mirror, my mask was complete. I was put together on the outside, but on the inside, I was broken. It was approaching 11 p.m., so I walked over to the pregame party to meet my friends. Greeting everyone and wearing a big smile, for all they knew, my life was perfect. Appearances can be so deceiving.

I had just started college at Sam Houston University, where I received a scholarship to play Division 1 soccer. Soccer ruled my whole life—from age two on. I missed out on countless events for soccer like the births of my loved ones, church, social gatherings, and at times, even school itself. It didn't matter though because I loved it. It's who I was and I was proud of it.

I grew up in a loving home that placed a large emphasis on success and achievement. My parents expected excellence, and that's what I strived for—not only in soccer, but in everything I did. I graduated with my associates degree a week before I graduated high school, and I was thriving, confident in who I was, and knew where I was going. That is, until my freshman year of college pulled the rug out from under me. From there, I experienced many highs and lows. My college years felt like a roller coaster of emotions, and I frequently tried to avoid the ups and downs.

Riding that roller coaster, I often found myself thinking, *Why didn't anyone warn me of the pressures I'd soon be under? Why didn't anyone warn me of the feelings of inadequacy that would come? Why didn't anyone warn me of the battlefield I'd experienced in my mind? Why didn't anyone tell me that no matter how hard I try, I'll still fall short? Why didn't anyone tell me that I placed my hope in something that would never last?*

I thought, *I must be the only one who feels this way.* Everybody around me seemed to be living their best life, but then I realized some of them were wearing a mask too.

According to the American College Health Association's National College Health Assessment (NCHA) in 2020, 53% of college students reported feeling hopeless. Dr. Joe Rubino estimates that approximately 85% of people worldwide struggle with self-esteem issues. A 2020 study by the UK government found that 61% of adults and 66% of children felt negative or very negative about their body image most of the time. Additionally, a Harvard study revealed that nearly three in five young adults felt they lacked "meaning or purpose" in their lives, and half of them reported that their mental health was negatively impacted by "not knowing what to do with my life."[1]

When I graduated college, I had a master's degree in business administration, and I had just played my last year of soccer as captain at Sam Houston. Even after all of those achievements, one problem still remained: I didn't know who I was anymore. My whole life had been about soccer and making good grades, and now what? I had no idea where to go. How was I supposed to know what I wanted to do for the rest of my life? *What if I don't know enough? I definitely don't have enough experience. What if soccer is all I'm good at, and now my best days are behind me?* As I looked around after graduation, holding my master's degree, I expected to feel a lasting sense of accomplishment. Instead, it was fleeting. Now, I had no idea where I fit into this world.

When I got back home to Dallas, I began going out every weekend and then attending church on Sundays. The more I thought about my life, the more I didn't know what my purpose was anymore. I was begging for *anyone* to tell me what I should do and looking for *anything* to fill the hole in my heart. I've never felt so disconnected from my true self before. It's like looking into a mirror and seeing my reflection shattered by the weight of everything I'd swept under the rug. Instead of seeing myself, I saw only missing pieces, and I didn't know where they came from or how to put them back together.

I couldn't explain it to anybody either because I didn't understand it myself. Every time I tried to express my feelings, people would discount them with comments like, "You know you are pretty," "You obviously have a nice body; you just want attention," "You have a master's degree; you should know any job would be lucky to have you," or "You've had a great life; what could you possibly be upset about?" Frustrated, I wanted to scream back, "I know I should know this, but I don't!" "I know I've had a great life, and I am grateful for it, but there is still something missing!"

Comments like these made me feel like something was wrong with me for having feelings of inadequacy, which led me to try to ignore them even more. I felt dumb for feeling the way I did, so I pretended they didn't exist. Going out, drinking, and getting attention from guys made me feel good about myself for a moment, but it never lasted. Eventually, that got old too, and my heart continued to long for something more. I never could have imagined I would actually find it.

One night, I felt like I hit rock bottom and God met me right where I was. So, I decided to give God one year of my life. No more half in the world and half in church. I was going all in with God. Whatever He told me to do, I was determined to follow through and see if it made a difference in my life. I decided, *If it doesn't work, I'll just go back to living as I always have. But if it does, I have everything to gain.*

It turned out to be the best decision I have ever made. God took me on a beautiful journey—a journey where I found hope. A hope that lasts. A hope that's trustworthy. A hope that will never let me down. My wander to belong is over. My wander to discover if I had a purpose is over. All of the pieces of me that I lost along the way, He restored. He put me back together in such a beautiful way—a better way. God made me new. I'm no longer broken. My worth is no longer fluctuating, seeking approval from external things because I found who I am, my true identity. I am fully known and loved; there is no further reason to strive or hide. I am proud of the person I am and I feel free. The pressures that once weighed me down have lifted. Now, I know I am the right girl, not because of me, but because of who lives inside of me. My healing journey was not always easy, but I would do it all over again because I know how full my heart is now, and yours can be too.

During those confusing times, I wish somebody would have been vulnerable enough to share their experiences with me—the truth behind the highlight reels so I didn't feel completely alone. Therefore, I'm sharing my experiences and my healing journey through faith in God and counseling to bring light to these dark spaces.

Maybe you picked up this book today because you're tired of putting your identity in the wrong things and coming up short. Maybe you picked it up because the lies you believe about yourself have been holding you back, and you don't know where to go from here. Maybe you simply liked the cover and felt intrigued. Whatever the reason, my hope is that through sharing my journey and experiences, you find encouragement to seek God with all your heart and you begin living in the freedom Jesus died for. Discovering the truth about who you are in Him will provide a hope that never fails and a foundation that will never let you down.

You need to know you *are* enough and you have a purpose in your life. As you continue to read this book, I pray the lies of the enemy are exposed, every limiting belief is stripped away, and you begin to step into the fullness of who God created you to be. I know God is going to meet you right where you are just as He did for me.

CHAPTER 2

BREAKDOWN OR BREAKTHROUGH

I sat for hours crying in my car feeling like a failure. I'd worked my whole life for this, and my family had invested so much time and money into it. The reality of my dream had become a nightmare. *Nothing is going how I expected it to.* I felt like I had let us all down. *How am I supposed to recover from this? I made a mistake coming here. I should just go home.*

I came to college with such high hopes, as did many others. Our hopes were found in a plethora of different areas. It's common for people to place their hope in things where they feel worthy or valuable. For some, it's a job, grades, looks, or relationships, but for me primarily it was a sport—soccer to be specific. I mean, how could I not? It was all I'd known from a young age. I put my heart and soul into the game, not to mention the huge time commitment. Most of my upbringing was spent on the soccer field. Driving two hours round trip to practice four times a week and then playing games on the weekends was my normal routine.

My parents put me in soccer as soon as I could walk. By the time I was three years old, I was already in a league with kids who were two or more years older than me. I had a natural talent and everyone around me affirmed it. I never questioned my ability or my place on the soccer field—I knew I belonged there. It was my identity. My whole life, the goal had been to play Division 1 soccer in college and possibly to pursue a professional career. I traveled all across the country to play. Everything else took a backseat to soccer, and it was paying off.

When I was 14, I was invited to the Mexican National Team soccer camp and was being recruited by several Division 1 schools. I committed to one of them during my sophomore year of high school. By my senior year, I was playing on a semi-pro team. My dream of becoming a professional soccer player seemed within reach. I felt worthy and valuable because of the recognition and success I had achieved. I never imagined the game would let me down, but after my first college semester, hopelessness set in. That is, until I learned to put my hope in the only One who'll never let me down: Jesus.

Without Jesus, I would have allowed my circumstance to define me as a failure and missed out on a powerful testimony that awaited me if I chose to stay.

Soccer, along with a few other sports, required us to be on my new college campus, Sam Houston, by July for summer workouts. I met a guy right when I got there who also played a sport, whom I'll call Brad. He asked for my number and texted me that night. After a few messages, I made it clear by saying, "Just so you know, I don't want to get into a relationship right now." I wanted to find my place at the college before jumping into anything, plus I didn't find him particularly attractive.

Despite that, we ended up texting all day, every day, for about a month. Without a conscious awareness or my permission, something shifted for me: I started to catch feelings. I didn't realize it until it was too late. We went to the same party and kissed. I was on cloud nine when I went to sleep that night, fulfilled and excited for the memories college would bring. The next day, I felt giddy and waited for my phone to ring, but it never did. With every check of my phone, the rejection hit deeper. He ghosted me for three days...not a word. My fragile freshman heart was broken and quite frankly a little embarrassed. How could I let myself catch feelings for a man who would do this? A man I didn't even find attractive to begin with. *I just want to know what happened.*

We later saw each other at a student-athlete event. The way he avoided eye contact with me was almost impressive. Even without speaking, the tension was thick; I felt it, and I knew he did too. We didn't say a word to each other, but that night, he texted me, likely to avoid another awkward encounter like the one earlier. He told me he didn't want a relationship. I was confused by the sudden change of heart. I was used to being the one not interested in dating someone, so this bruised my ego and left me perplexed. I hate to admit it, but him not wanting to be with me just made me want to be with him more.

I never like to show my emotions; my default is often to pretend everything is great and that I don't care. I was hurt though, so I responded with, "I told you a month ago I didn't want a relationship with you either," and then we stopped talking. The next time my friends and I went out, I knew he would be there. So, I took my time getting ready and tried to look super cute. He needed to see what he was missing out on and needed to know that us not being together didn't phase me. I flirted with other guys right in front of him and made sure he saw that I was having a good time.

At that moment, I didn't realize I was trying to prove my worth by showing that other guys were interested in me. I was attempting to validate my value to him by demonstrating that others saw me as desirable. Trying to get his attention, I was even posting on my Snapchat story about a show we used to talk about, hoping he would slide up.

The ironic part is, I didn't even like him to begin with, and now I was the only one who cared. How did that happen? Outwardly, I seemed unaffected because I pretended I didn't care. What I didn't realize was that while

I was protecting my outward appearance, I was actually invalidating and not processing the emotions I was feeling inside.

Later, I asked myself, *Why is it so important for this particular guy to want to be with me?* Even if everyone else in the room was showing interest, all I wanted was to understand why *he didn't*.

The truth is, I didn't have strong feelings for him. What his rejection revealed was a deeper insecurity within me— one that made me seek his affirmation to fill the void I was feeling. I thought I needed his affirmation in order to feel secure about myself.

It was a pivotal moment in my life when I found my security and worth in God. It changed how I respond to rejection. It still hurts and I have to bring those real human emotions to God, but it doesn't send me in a spiral anymore of needing that person to change their mind about me in order for me to know I really am worthy.

Now, I understand I have nothing to prove to anyone, and neither do you. You are enough simply because you are a child of God, period. Just because someone couldn't see your worth doesn't mean you are not valuable. One person's lack of interest doesn't mean you are unwanted, and one person's failure to love you doesn't make you unlovable. I no longer feel the need to prove my value to a guy to believe it myself because I have allowed the truth of who I am to fill the gaps left by my previous insecurities. If someone doesn't appreciate me, it simply means they weren't meant for me. Their opinion doesn't change the truth of my worth, and it doesn't change yours either.

Luckily for me, preseason was starting, and like I've mentioned, I've always put soccer first. Everything else in my life took a back seat, so I didn't give this boy another thought. Soccer was the perfect distraction. Summer training went very well, and I was so excited for our fall season to start. Part of the reason I chose to commit to play at Sam Houston was because the coach said I would be able to come in and make an immediate impact. That was important for me, and I trusted his word, so you can imagine my surprise when the promises made came up empty. The max I played my freshman year was 15 minutes a game. I went from playing every moment growing up, to hardly playing at all!

Since I'm not one to give up easily, I was determined to prove myself to my coach, giving my all in every practice and during any minutes he gave me in the game. It was challenging because I received overwhelming support from parents and players, with comments like, "I don't know why you're not playing more," or "Our team plays better when you're on the field." While I was thankful for these comments, at the end of the day, only one person's opinion mattered, and he wouldn't give me the time of day. I would have understood if we were winning every game without me on the field, but we were struggling. I felt so unseen and didn't know what to do. The question, *Why am I here?* consumed my thoughts.

I didn't want to have any regrets, so I scheduled a meeting with the coach. Big mistake. I asked him if there was anything specific I could work on to get more playing time. His exact words were, "To be blunt, you're just not as good as the other girls. You will never play holding (defensive mid), and I'm not sure you can run that long." God must have given me His strength in that moment because all I wanted to do was cry. Instead, I looked right back at him and said, "Well, you're not going to know unless you try."

I left feeling hopeless and defeated. Rejection from Brad was painful, but it was easier to move past because I had soccer. Now, even soccer—the one thing I always relied on and where I knew I was good enough—was being questioned. I was left with a paralyzing thought: *Maybe I don't have what it takes after all.* If I wasn't good enough for soccer—the one thing I had always excelled in—then what was I good enough for? This doubt began to seep into every area of my life, making me question everything, including my worth and purpose.

So, there I was, crying in my car for hours, feeling like such a failure. I thought about all the hard work, the time spent, and other things I missed in life for this dream, not to mention my family's investment of their time and money. *I'm letting everyone down.* In the next few games, my time on the field was cut altogether, and I didn't play at all. The hardest part wasn't just not getting to play, it was looking into the stands and seeing my parents, feeling like I had failed them. Even growing up, if I received a trophy that

13

wasn't 1st place, I didn't want to take it home. Not out of arrogance, but because I truly didn't believe I deserved it. My performance wasn't good enough, so I felt like *I wasn't good enough*.

The sad part is, I don't hold anybody else to this standard except for myself, so that should've clued me in that something was wrong. My parents were so encouraging, which I appreciated greatly, but I knew they thought I should be playing. No matter how hard I tried, I still fell short. I felt so much shame. I told my parents not to invite anybody to my games. Every game I didn't play or played minimal minutes, I tried to pretend the best I could that it didn't bother me too much so they didn't worry about me, but inside I was breaking. It wasn't just being benched, it was the team environment as a whole. It was toxic.

I would come to practice with a smile on my face, ready to tackle the day's training. But as practices continued, my smile gradually faded until it disappeared entirely. The coaches were far from encouraging. I remember when one game changed everything. After a tough loss, we were on the bus ride home, talking and trying to move on, not letting the loss bring us down. Suddenly, our assistant coach stood up and yelled at us. I've never seen such anger in someone's eyes before. She walked up and down the aisle, angrily telling us we weren't allowed to talk, laugh, or smile. We were required to sit in silence for the next hour, and at the next training session, we weren't allowed to speak during the warm-up.

So much for soccer being a great escape! Now, I lived in constant fear that I'd make the wrong move. Soccer being fun wasn't even in the realm of possibility anymore. Our coach started calling us out individually for everything wrong. I couldn't go to practice without hearing my name be called what felt like a million times. At this point, I felt like I couldn't do anything right. *I hate it here.*

I was already struggling with feeling like I didn't belong, and a teammate seemed determined to make it worse. Whenever I spoke in the locker room, on the field, or on the bus, she would say, "Shut up, Ashley." I had no idea why I was her target for belittlement. Sometimes, other players would join in as a joke, which only made me feel more powerless. How could I find my voice when I was already at a loss for where I fit in?

On top of that, I was trying to find my footing with balancing school and soccer. I was missing a lot of class for away games, and the workload was heavier than I was used to. I was overwhelmed and stressed because I didn't want to fail at this too. I was already failing in soccer, so really I needed to succeed academically to prove to myself that I wasn't a failure. Good grades came easily in high school, but I was so anxious about passing my college classes that I would do anything to pass...even cheat if I had to.

Let me share some thoughts on this for a moment. I realized that in the long run, I was only cheating myself. By giving myself an out, I wasn't forced to learn some of the material I could use today. When we take the short cuts, we have to spend time learning things we should already know. I'm experiencing this reality now.

The academic and schedule challenges also created an opening for the enemy to make me believe I am not good enough and make me believe I have limitations that I actually don't have. The truth is, just because something doesn't come easy doesn't mean I am dumb and don't belong. It means I am learning a new subject and I need to give myself time and grace to learn it. Learning new things is uncomfortable and stretches us, but it ultimately makes us grow. I've had my fair share of breakdowns over one of my classes and questioned if this was really for me. But when you stand on the other side of it, you realize it *was* worth it all along.

Whether I pass or fail, it doesn't define me. I actually learn more from my failures than my successes. It's more rewarding and fulfilling to put in the hours and pass on your own, no matter how many times it takes, than to cheat and get something you didn't earn. Doing it the right way shows you have integrity, which builds trust and confidence in yourself and others. Cheating may get you short-term success, but having integrity leads to long-term success because your success is built on a solid foundation and empowers you to believe in yourself.

When you get into the workforce, if you don't grasp a new concept quickly, will you just give up and quit because it's hard? My answer is no, but that's what I was training myself to do in college every time I took the easy way out in class because I didn't think I could do it on my own or I was being lazy. The greatest thing I could have done for my future self was to create healthy patterns while I was in school, developing good study techniques. This would have helped me avoid some of the mental battles with doubts in my own abilities in my career and discounting myself because of self-imposed limitations. But there's great news! If you don't have good patterns in your life right now, you can choose to change them today, and your future self will thank you.

Now, back to my first soccer season. Throughout the semester, I had multiple phone calls with my mom, telling her that I was done with soccer after the season and planned to leave Sam Houston. I would say, "I am done after this season. I don't want to be here anymore." She always responded with, "Ashley, just see how the rest of the year goes. You don't have to make that decision now." This frustrated me because it felt like she wasn't supporting my decision. I would reply, "I have to go," and hang up. I wasn't busy; I just didn't want to continue the conversation. In reality, she was supporting me, just not in the way I wanted. I wanted her to say, "Yeah, come home," but she believed I wasn't ready to give up. Honestly, I kept having the conversation because no matter how many times I said it, I couldn't completely shut the door either.

Later, I realized that I couldn't fully close the door because I was trying to force what I wanted, even though it wasn't aligned with God's will. As a result, I lacked the peace that comes from following His path. When you don't know what to do, following God's way will always bring you peace. Having someone to discuss these major decisions with can prevent you from making rash choices based on fleeting feelings that you might regret later. I am beyond grateful that I had my mom. Despite my frustrations and sometimes taking them out on her, she continued to love and support me. I appreciate her honesty, even if I didn't fully value it at the time.

The unknown was a burden I carried with me. I desperately wanted to leave college, but what if I was supposed to stay? Full of fear, I worried that I would make the wrong decision and regret it. I had many breakdowns, but I didn't stay in self-pity. I wrestled with God on what I should do, telling Him all the reasons why I should leave. I made declarative statements like "I am going to quit because..." "I am going to go home because..." Still, I was left with no peace. *Should I stay, or should I leave?* I kept having the same conversation with God, until I finally got tired. "You know what God? I'll do whatever You want me to do. If You want me to go, which I strongly recommend, then I'll go, but if You want me to stay, then I will stay."

This was the first time I actually surrendered the choice to God and was really okay with either answer. I definitely wanted Him to say *go*, but I was okay if He said to stay.

Because I was finally okay with either outcome, that's when God's voice became clear. It's hard to hear God's voice when your emotions are heightened, because then you only hear what you want to hear. Every reason I had to leave, He countered with a reason to stay. I asked, "Is it even worth it?" He replied, "I'm trying to teach you something; I'm preparing you for something." I asked, "Will soccer be different next year?" He said, "Trust Me."

Right after I had the revelation that God was asking me to stay, I heard a sermon that really solidified my decision and gave me the confidence that I did hear Him correctly. I know he was preaching to a whole congregation, but I am convinced the pastor's word was just for me. It felt like this pastor must have been eavesdropping on my conversation with God. This was pivotal for me; it confirmed what I felt like God was already speaking. It was exactly what I needed to feel secure in my decision to not quit because logically it made no sense to stay. The main message of the sermon was not to give up prematurely. When you plant a seed, it has to grow roots before it grows upward. If the plant had no roots, it wouldn't be able to withstand any type of inclement weather. The deeper the roots, the stronger the plant and the more weather it can withstand.

Similarly, when we are in seasons of feeling hidden, unseen, or undervalued, we are like a seed. God is developing our roots and character so when He elevates us we are prepared. It is essential to have strong enough roots to withstand what God wants to build. The problem is, most people never stay long enough to have their breakthrough. They continue to move from place to place when opposition comes and are surprised when their same problem keeps showing up with a different face. Stay planted in the place God called you so you don't miss the harvest He wants to bring on the other side of your obedience. You need a word from God you can stand on because it'll take time. It'll appear like nothing is changing. Pastor Michael pointed out, "The place of death and the place of destiny look the same for a season." Then, all of a sudden, you shoot up tall and get to experience the harvest of stewarding the word God gave you well.

This wasn't at all what I imagined my first year of college would look like, and maybe you find yourself in a similar season, questioning why things haven't turned out as you expected. Maybe you worked hard for something and have nothing to show for it. Maybe school is miserable for you. Maybe people at work don't value you. Maybe you have family members, classmates, or coworkers who degrade you. Maybe you've placed your hope in something that's failing you. It may feel like the season you're in is hopeless and never-ending. It's hard when it seems like nobody sees, understands, or appreciates you. Why continue if nobody cares? The enemy would like you to believe it's always going to be this way, but I'm here to tell you it's not over. God sees you, understands you, values you, and will deliver you. Don't let a difficult chapter in your life define your entire life. We serve a God of restoration and redemption who can turn any situation into a stepping stone toward the promises He has for your life.

The great news is that you can find peace and joy while waiting for God to change your circumstances. All you need to do is shift your focus.

As Romans 8:6 (NIV) says, "The mind governed by the flesh is death, but the mind governed by the Spirit is life and peace." The enemy wants you to focus on being the victim, what's going wrong, and what you lack because it leads to a kind of death—not a physical death, but a life filled with misery on earth. His goal is to make you believe the plans and purposes God has for you are dead. Remember, death and destiny look the same for a season, and you get to choose who you come into agreement with. Will it be Satan, the father of lies, or God, the One who cannot lie? The Bible tells us Abraham believed in what God promised him and "it was accounted to him for righteousness." Meaning, as soon as Abraham believed in the promise God made to him, it was his. He didn't get it right away, but it's like the promise was in transit, and at the perfect time he would receive it if he did not move out of God's will and give up prematurely.

Instead of focusing on what's wrong, meditate on what God says and ask Him, "How can You use me here?" or "What are You teaching me here?" God will ultimately deliver you from these difficulties, but don't overlook the opportunities for growth and impact during the waiting period.

In the Bible, Joseph had a grand vision for his life, but nothing went according to his plan. He was betrayed and sold into slavery by his brothers, then falsely accused of sleeping with his employer's wife and thrown into prison. I imagine I'd feel hopeless, disappointed, hurt, and frustrated in his situation. Yet, Joseph knew God's character was good and trusted His faithfulness. Even while being treated unfairly, Joseph chose to serve faithfully where he was, and God made his way prosperous. Suddenly, Joseph went from being a slave to becoming second in command over all of Egypt. Though it seemed sudden, God used every step of Joseph's journey to fulfill His plan for his life.

And God is doing the same for your life. I know it doesn't look the way you thought it would, but I want to encourage you: your plan may have failed, but God's plan will never fail. You will experience a "suddenly" moment where God changes everything and you see the harvest you've been longing for *if* you remain steadfast and unmovable despite what the enemy throws your way. Jesus was pierced and bruised for us, but He was never broken. In the same way, life may bruise or afflict us, but it will not be the end of us. You are a conqueror in Christ Jesus. You are not just fighting for victory; you are coming from victory. The key is to wait on the Lord with expectancy and assurance that you will see His goodness manifest in your life. When your focus is on Him, nothing can stand in the way of what God has in store for your life. He is the only hope that will never fail. It may take time, but no season is wasted with God.

It didn't make logical sense to stay on my team and expect things to be different. The people playing over me would still be there, plus another outstanding player was coming back to play in my position. All things considered, the odds were definitely stacked against me. But I had a word from God, and that changed everything. I had peace in staying and knew my breakthrough was coming, so I stayed. Peace didn't come from having all the answers or understanding why things were happening. It came when I surrendered and trusted the One who does: Jesus.

God continued to shift my perspective that year and soften my heart. I realized that while I don't get to choose the cards I'm dealt, I do get to control my attitude. I may feel like I have it bad, but some people might see me as the luckiest person in the world. There are people who could only dream of attending college or playing the sport they love. I was reminded to return to a heart of gratitude and recognize the blessings already in my life.

With that being said, you can be grateful for everything you have and still have a longing for more. Why? Because God created you for more. There is nothing wrong with that. The key is to remain expectant for all that God has destined for you without rushing ahead and allowing it to steal your peace or joy in the place you're currently in.

Yes, things didn't go as I expected, and yes, the coach was treating me unfairly, but that was only a small part of my day. Regardless of what's happening, there is always something to smile about. I love the saying, "Is the glass half empty or half full?" It begs the question: do you want to live your life miserable by focusing only on the negatives? Of course not. Nobody wants to live that way. The more you focus on the good in your life, the more you will appreciate it.

After I made the choice to stay, I chose to just play for myself. I didn't worry about the other voices or the outcome. I just played and appreciated what I did have. The coach's words suddenly held no weight over me. I went from merely going through the motions to embracing each day. It had been a long time since I felt genuinely happy—not just fleeting moments, but lasting contentment. I made it through the storm, but only because I wasn't alone. The more I focused on the present day, the easier the days got. Before I knew it, weeks flew by. Those weeks turned into months. What felt impossible now felt like a breeze. Not only did I make it through that difficult season, but I made it with a smile. I was happy.

At the end of our spring season, we found out our assistant coach was leaving. I could already see glimpses of God making a way where there seemed to be no way for a better experience for me next year.

If I expected God to do His part, I needed to do mine. That summer, I met with a trainer almost every day to ensure I was in the best shape possible. I also worked with a skills coach twice a week to keep my technique sharp and played with a summer team. If God was going to make a way, I wanted to be prepared for the opportunity...and I was.

By the time preseason was over my sophomore year, I had my breakthrough. I was starting and playing most, if not all, of the game. Ironically, the position I was playing was holding mid– the position they told me I'd never play. I was able to prove everybody who doubted me wrong because I was obedient and didn't give up. I learned to have a new appreciation for the time I was able to have on the field and never took it for granted. I'm so thankful that God told me to stay and gave me the strength to do it. Only God can completely turn things around when there seems to be no way. If I had left because things got tough, I would have missed out on the incredible harvest I experienced in soccer the following few years. I loved my next three years playing soccer at Sam Houston. Although it was extremely hard, I wouldn't change my freshman year experience because I can now see the fruits of what it developed in me.

I learned sometimes we go through trials even when we are in the will of God. It's not because of something we did wrong; it's just the result of living in a fallen world. As it says in James 1:2–4 (NIV): "Consider it pure joy, my brothers and sisters, whenever you face trials of many kinds, because you know that the testing of your faith produces perseverance. Let perseverance finish its work so that you may be mature and complete, not lacking anything."

Reflecting on the challenges I faced with my coach and the overall environment, I can see that I was in the will of God, yet I still faced trials. God used these experiences to develop valuable qualities within me. During the trial, it was difficult and painful, but looking back, I am glad it happened. These experiences taught me to rely on God and overcome adversity. I even had a back injury I thought would never fully heal, but after that year, the pain never returned.

God also used the trials later, when I became team captain. I was able to lead with compassion because I knew firsthand what it felt like to be the one not getting any minutes. My experiences gave me a perspective I wouldn't have had otherwise.

I remember how much it hurt to hear players who were on the field the whole game say they didn't care about soccer or didn't feel like playing, especially when I wanted so desperately to be out there. It felt like a slap in the face. It was infuriating to see them break team rules and still get to play or skip summer workouts with no consequences while I was putting in the hard work and following the rules. It's difficult to stay motivated when bad behavior seems to be rewarded.

I could have used this as an excuse to follow suit, but I decided I didn't want my character to be influenced by what was happening around me. Instead, I chose to focus on what I could control: my effort. I made it a point to always give 100% in every practice, every conditioning session, and every game. When the tables turned and I was given the chance to play, I continued to give my all. This wasn't just because I expected it of myself, but also because I wanted to honor the opportunity I had and show respect to my teammates. I didn't want to contribute to any sense of entitlement or disrespect they may have felt from other players or staff. By never taking any minutes for granted and giving my all every time, I demonstrated respect for every player on the field. Although everybody wants to be playing and that part still stings, it's always easier to support and celebrate others when you know they put in the work too and take it seriously, so I made sure I always did.

Another challenge of not playing was "Load Day"—the day after a game when players who didn't get much field time would have an intense practice, while those who had played would recover with stretches and rolling. The goal was to maintain the same fitness levels across the team, and while this practice was valid, the problem arose when the recovering players would talk and laugh on the sidelines, seemingly oblivious to the hard work of their teammates.

When I transitioned to the recovery side of Load Day, I, along with some other players, made a conscious effort to cheer and support those who were working hard, just as

27

they had supported me during the game. These small changes made a significant impact on the team's morale. Demonstrating support and valuing each member's effort truly strengthened the entire organization.

I distinctly felt a shift in how some people treated me once I started playing, compared to when I wasn't, and I didn't like it at all. It made me feel like I wasn't important unless I played, which is discouraging. The team needed to cultivate a culture that recognized the importance of every member's contribution, even if they didn't play a single minute in a game. Without the efforts of all players in practice, the team wouldn't be as well prepared. The energy and encouragement from the sidelines can push teammates past fatigue and change the game's trajectory. High energy from substitutes, for example, can make a significant difference. Every member plays a vital role, and I truly believe each player contributes to the team's success whether they are on the field or not. The key is recognizing and valuing each contribution. Ultimately, everyone wants to understand their role and how they add value to the organization. It's the leader's responsibility to ensure that team members know their contributions matter. I did my best to lead with this in mind.

This experience is a testament to the truth that no season is wasted with God. He can use everything you've gone through in one season to benefit another. While He doesn't cause bad things to happen, He will use them for your good, developing qualities in you to prepare you for what He has in store for you.

CHAPTER 3

THE B'S THAT AFFECT SELF-WORTH

There are times when we face trials as a result of our choice to live outside of God's will for our lives. The hardships I encountered in the years that followed were largely due to me living on my own terms, rather than aligning with God's Word. Part of me loved Jesus, while the other part was entangled in worldly pursuits.

I was going to church and a Bible study weekly, but I also had my weekly margaritas before heading to the club. At first, I felt guilty for going out and getting drunk, but eventually, those feelings subsided. A lot of my friends were Christians and they were doing it too, so I really didn't see the problem. *They're doing it, so it must be okay.* Even as a new Christian I knew the Bible said not to get drunk, but I didn't understand why. I liked drinking with my friends and dancing the night away at the club. It seemed harmless to me at the time, but I didn't realize the repercussions happening beneath the surface until after I graduated college.

Soccer was going well, so I got my confidence back and was thriving in my sophomore year. However, with influences all around me and my parents not there to keep me in check and remind me of who I was supposed to be, things began to shift. I knew my values, but without understanding the reasons behind them, they were easy to deviate from, especially by looking to those around me to determine what was "acceptable." It started with small compromises, and before I knew it, I was questioning my self-worth. *How did I get here?*

There are many things that can affect one's self-worth. I am going to highlight the four that I personally experienced.

Besties

Proverbs 12:26 (NKJV): "The righteous should choose his friends carefully, For the way of the wicked leads them astray."

Who you choose to surround yourself with impacts the direction your life is headed. An unknown author famously said, "Show me who your friends are, and I'll show you your future." Friends can be a huge asset to your life or a huge liability. Your closest friends can build you up, call you higher, and push you toward God, or they can tear you down, encourage bad behavior, and push you further from

God. If your friends take studying seriously, you are more likely to study more. If your friends treat school as an option, you're more likely to slack off. The more you spend time with someone, the more you adopt their attitude and behaviors…for better or worse.

Your friendships shape you in ways you don't even realize. A negative friend is someone who puts you down or constantly puts you in bad situations. These types of friends will hinder your growth and success. A positive friend is someone who supports you, empowers you, and motivates you. They want you to succeed and believe you can do it, which gives you more confidence to pursue your dreams. Ultimately, you have the power to choose your friends and the kind of influences you want in your life, so you can't use other people as an excuse for your shortcomings. A solid rule of thumb is if you wouldn't trade places with them, don't seek advice from them. If you want study tips, don't ask a friend who is failing their class for study tips. If you want a good healthy marriage, don't ask someone who has been divorced three times for marriage advice. Ask somebody who has a healthy marriage like you would want to have.

I didn't put much thought into who I surrounded myself with when I got to college because I didn't understand the magnitude of the effect others could have on my life. I figured *whoever I hit it off with will become my friends*. Luckily, I got some incredible friends this way, but I also had some who led me astray. I adopted some unhealthy mindsets from a few people, and it wasn't until I distanced myself from them when I realized the effect they had on my life. I realized my actions were not aligning with the vision I had for my future and had to face the reality that you don't just wake up one day and have the life you want. It comes from being intentional with the choices you make and ensuring they align with the direction you want your life to go. You get to determine whether the vision God has given you for your life remains a dream or becomes a reality through the choices you make daily. A big part of this is choosing to surround yourself with the right kind of people. Some of my insecurity was directly influenced by people I spent a lot of time with.

Booze

Most college kids have had their fair share of drunken nights. I know I have. I loved going out. If you asked me if there was any harm in getting wasted, I would have responded *no*. As long as you're safe and you have a designated driver, have fun!

My first time going out in college, I didn't know what I was getting myself into. The soccer team was all going to meet up and go to Shenaniganz. Where I am from, that is a fun center with arcade games, bowling, laser tag, and go-karts, so I showed up dressed for that kind of activity. I walk in the door, and imagine my surprise when everybody else was wearing short skirts, crop tops, and booties. *They really dressed up for some bowling.* I laughed quietly to myself and made a mental note. *Buy some crop tops and booties.* Not matching the clothes vibe is always the worst, but I quickly got over it when my song "No Hands" came on. It's quite literally impossible for me to ignore the dance floor. Although, there wasn't a proper dance floor in the apartment we met at before our night out, so the living room sufficed. "The Uber is on the way," I heard someone say from across the room. "Time for shots." Vodka shots lined the table. Bottoms up! Welcome to college.

We arrived at Shenaniganz, and I was feeling good. *I know my vision is a little blurry, but are my eyes deceiving me this bad?* Instead of arcade fun, we were at a club. The club had the best of both worlds: country on one side and hip hop on the other. The dance floor was calling, and it would've been wrong to ignore the call. Jaw dropping at what I saw quickly turned into me dropping it to the actual floor. *I feel great. College is going to be so fun!*

It was thrilling at first, but eventually it got old. Bad things seem to always accompany excessive alcohol because your decision-making skills are impaired, leading you to make choices you're significantly less likely to make sober.

Being under the influence—whether through drinking, drugs, or lust—makes you more susceptible to the enemy's manipulations. First Peter 5:8 (NIV) warns, "Be alert and of sober mind. Your enemy the devil prowls around like a roaring lion looking for someone to devour." The enemy is always watching, ready to attack. He places temptations in your mind, making them seem like the best idea ever, only to condemn you the next day and make you feel like the worst person for doing it. It's like convincing a child that stealing candy is thrilling and cool, then turning around and telling them they're a terrible person who will never amount to anything. Satan's goal is to lead you into bad decisions, then make you feel as small, ashamed, and worthless as possible. His goal is to keep you from reaching your full potential.

By being sober, you're automatically more aware, making it easier to resist the enemy's temptations. Choosing to be under the influence gives the enemy an opening to distract, deceive, or discourage you from where God wants to take you. Often people choose to drink excessively or participate in drugs because they want to escape their thoughts, numb their pain, or fill the void in their hearts. These things are an unfulfilling counterfeit to the legitimate needs people are actually searching for.

It's ironic how we often crave control, yet so easily relinquish it by indulging in booze or pills. This will always lead you down a path that ultimately leaves you feeling empty and searching for a greater high or endorphin rush. The only way to be truly fulfilled and have relief from your racing thoughts, without the negative consequences, is to surrender your life to Jesus. He is where the joy is, He is where the peace is, and He is where the love is.

Boys

As I previously mentioned, poor choices tend to accompany excessive alcohol. I fell prey to this more times than I care to admit. Alcohol really just became an excuse to do whatever I wanted to do. Most of my friends were in committed relationships, so they would hang out with their boyfriends and leave us single people to be bored alone. I got close with a girl who was also single, and she made everything sound like a great idea. I learned how to enjoy being single from her. It was the mindset of just have fun, until you find the one. This entailed kissing a random guy at the bar or having "a roster." Apparently, the phrase *having a roster* originated from guys having a list of women they could call up anytime for casual sex.

I always wanted to wait until marriage to have sex, so I had my own definition of what this meant. Even here you can see the battle I was fighting between my flesh, living in the world, and my spirit, living for Jesus. I defined having a roster as texting or hanging out casually with multiple guys and entertaining them even though I knew I would never be with them. The idea is just have fun and pass the time, until someone you actually like comes along. The guys I did this with were big time players, so I knew they weren't dateable anyway. I honestly didn't see any harm in it if we both led with clarity, but the harm done was revealed over time; I found myself questioning if I'd ever be good enough for someone to choose—someone I'd actually want to be with. One of my greatest desires is to have a God-fearing man as my husband and to be a mom, so this fear felt paralyzing. Eventually, it made me be overly obsessed with how I looked and how I "should act" so I'd be worth it.

The waters got muddied because I got emotionally attached to a few different guys over the years who did not have the qualities and values I would want in a husband. The more you hang out with someone one on one alone, it is inevitable someone is bound to catch feelings or get emotionally attached. When feelings got involved, it made me lower my standards and compromise in some ways to please the guy I caught feelings for. I thought if I was easy going enough then he would commit to me. I didn't realize my idea of becoming low maintenance meant sacrificing my own needs, wants, and true desires to win a guy's affections. This was slowly lowering my self-esteem because I was teaching myself that my wants, needs, and desires were not important.

It was tricky. One particular guy and I would hang out all the time, but he technically never committed to me, so I didn't feel like I could expect more. In my mind, that's how I justified him bailing on plans, talking to other girls, or anything I normally would not be okay with. Originally, I was fine with hanging out with no commitment, but after things shifted in my heart, I just ended up getting hurt the more he wouldn't commit. I stayed because I could see the potential and thought I could change him. "You don't understand, he's different when he is with me." "When we are together, it's so good." More than that, I had a friend who would validate me and make excuses for the guy at every turn. "He's just scared to commit, but if he did it would obviously be with you," or "You can tell he likes you so much." I allowed him to treat me as an option when it was convenient rather than a priority as it should be. Really, I just needed a friend to be like, "Sorry, sis, he's not it." This may sting in the moment, but I would thank her for it later.

I needed someone to tell me the truth and remind me of my worth, so I'm here to do that for you. If you're in a situationship or with someone who treats you as anything less than the queen or king you are, this is your wake-up call. You deserve better, and you shouldn't accept being treated poorly. If they see you as an option, they don't deserve you at all. You are more precious than rubies. Understand your value: not just any person deserves you. Wait for the one who cherishes the rare gem that you are. Your future self will thank you for protecting your heart from unnecessary pain.

This unnecessary pain caused me to believe a lie that I wasn't good enough. Logically, I knew I was a catch and had a lot going for me, but subconsciously I was fighting a battle of, *What is it about me that doesn't seem to measure up? It feels like I'll never be the one who gets the happy ending.* An accumulation of having "harmless fun" with guys had turned into feeling rejected and doubting my worth. After college, God healed these parts of my heart and helped me see the truth.

Matthew 13:45–46 (AMP) says, "Again, the kingdom of heaven is like a merchant in search of fine pearls, and upon finding a single pearl of great value, he went and sold all that he had and bought it."

In this parable, the merchant finds a single pearl of great value and RECOGNIZES its worth. Many people could see the same pearl, yet not recognize the pearl's value. Just because everybody couldn't see the value in the pearl doesn't change the fact that the pearl always had great value. The merchant's response was to sell everything he had in order to have this one pearl because he knew what most people didn't have eyes to see. The one pearl far exceeded the value of everything he owned, so what the merchant gained in the one pearl surpassed the value of all he owned. The other people just simply missed out.

To be clear, this parable is illustrating that the Kingdom of God is far more valuable than anything in this world. Nothing comes close to a relationship with God, but the pearl also served as a great illustration of what I felt like God revealed to me about my own worth after college. After my self-worth had taken a hit from rejections, I was left with a crippling, lingering thought: *If these guys who don't even do the bare minimum don't want to commit to me, then what makes me think I'm going to be good enough for a godly man I actually desire to marry one day?* God healed those parts of me and revealed the lie I was believing. The truth is, God created me as a masterpiece. My worth and value does not change based on who has eyes to see it. Just as the pearl always had great value. so do I, and so do you. There will be people in your life who can't see it. It's not a *you* problem, it is a *them* problem. Instead of wasting your time convincing someone you are good enough, limit their access to you. It's not you who misses out, it's them.

If your goal when you go to an amusement park is to have someone to ride the rides with, don't take someone who hates riding rides. If you take someone who hates riding rides, you shouldn't be surprised when you have to ride the rides alone. The desire to want someone to ride with you is not wrong, but the expectation is just misplaced. They revealed to you they do not have the capability to meet your expectations, no matter how bad you want them to. If you expect more from someone who already revealed their intentions, then you are just going to be left disappointed and frustrated. Therefore, the desire or expectation isn't wrong; you just took the wrong person for the goal you had in mind.

In the same way, if my goal is to marry a God-fearing man, I shouldn't be entertaining guys who do not encompass that. Trying to expect more from a guy who does not embody the values and respect I would want from a man, is like asking a person who hates rides to the amusement park. It will just leave me hurt, frustrated, and disappointed because I am asking them to do something that's not in their character. My expectations and standards are not wrong or too high; they just have been misplaced on the wrong type of guys for the goal I have in mind. It's not that I wasn't good enough to love, I was just surrounding myself with guys who were just after lust. You cannot change someone, no matter how wonderful you are—only God can. Set yourself up for success and protect your heart by dating people who already have healthy patterns, rather than hoping to change potential.

On the flip side, I felt discouraged because it felt like I would never find what I truly wanted. I was fighting an inner battle because the guys who liked me and were great men didn't spark any feelings in me, while the ones I liked treated me as just an option. *Ugh, what's wrong with me? Why can't I catch feelings for the right type of guy?* I felt like I was going to have to settle, and I really didn't want to.

There was one guy, whom I'll call Tyler, who was my best friend and had great chemistry with. On paper, he was everything I ever could have wanted in a husband one day. It was difficult to navigate because I loved spending time with him yet, I couldn't shake the feeling that something was missing. Everyone around us said we should be together, and I felt immense pressure to make it work, even though I knew deep down I wasn't ready. I struggled because here was a man who seemed to have everything I wanted, yet I couldn't develop feelings for him. The same questions kept coming up. *Seriously, what's wrong with me? Why can't I let him in?* Deep down I knew with Tyler, it was different. He was someone who could really hurt me.

The next summer, I gave in. We started dating, and then we broke up a couple months later. He told me we couldn't be friends either afterward, which was my biggest fear all along. The next spring, I called him one day because I missed him, and we never stopped talking after that. This time I thought it was going to be different. We talked for months before we told anybody we were together because we wanted to figure things out on our own. I was happy. I thought he was going to be my end game.

To my surprise, his mom did not approve of our relationship and actively tried to separate us. This was confusing because our families were very close, and she had loved me before she knew we were dating. I couldn't take it anymore, so I asked him to talk to her. After he spoke with her, Tyler told me I needed to reach out to her as well. Although this irritated me, I swallowed my pride because I wanted our relationship to work. I texted her, but she responded with a harsh and distasteful message. I was furious and heartbroken. To sum it up, she felt like I wasn't good enough for her son.

This reaction triggered me deeply, and I immediately shut down. I sent the message to Tyler, hoping he would stand up for me. Instead, our emotions spiraled out of control, and we ended up breaking up. I was so angry that I never wanted to talk to him or his mom again. I didn't even grieve the breakup because all I felt was rage.

When my anger subsided, Tyler and I began talking as friends again. I was still upset with his mom and how everything had unfolded, so I believed in my heart we would never be together again.

Where I was at it seemed like I would have to choose between being with someone I was very attracted to and had feelings for *or* someone who shared my beliefs, would be a good husband, but I might not be in love with them. I felt like I was running out of time because there were only a handful of God-fearing men left, but I really didn't want to settle. I knew deep down there had to be something more, which made me search for it more, leaving me more disappointed each time the longing in my heart wasn't met.

Can someone like me really have it all? Will I ever find what I'm looking for? And if I did find this rare gem—a God-fearing man I found attractive—why would he choose me when there are so many other amazing women?

Even if a man had chosen me, would I have been able to let him in? I struggled to develop genuine feelings for real prospects because I couldn't fully open up to *anyone*. Part of the reason I spent time with guys who weren't good for me was that I knew they were emotionally unavailable, which somehow felt safer. I now realize it was because I had built walls around my heart that needed to come down before I could truly let anyone in. I had layers I needed to shed from morphing into who everybody expects me to be to get to the *real me*. I had to allow God to heal those parts of me before I could fully love myself and realize God did not make a mistake when He created me.

There's nothing wrong with my personality or my appearance. He made me the way I am on purpose for the purpose He has for my life. The man God has for me will love me for who I am. I won't need to change to make him happy. I don't have to dim my light to make him feel empowered. I won't be too much or not enough for him, and I won't have to feel like I'm begging him to stick around. The man God has for me will choose me too.

When I took myself out of these circles and quit entertaining guys just for fun, my self-worth returned. Now, I know what I deserve and I'm more careful to guard my heart because I refuse to settle for anything less than God's best for me. In the midst of waiting for God's best, I had to be real and ask myself, *Am I exhibiting the values and characteristics I am expecting my future spouse to possess?* If the answer is yes, then great. Galatians 6:9 says, "Do not grow weary in doing good for at the proper time you will reap a harvest if you do not give up." Keep doing what you should be doing, and at the perfect time God will bring the person into your life. Sometimes *you* are ready, but God is still preparing *them*. If the answer is no, develop those qualities. If you want a spouse who prays, be a person who prays. If you want a spouse who values fitness, be disciplined in your workouts. If you want a spouse who is generous, be a generous person. Cultivate the qualities you seek in a partner within yourself. As you focus on your personal growth and become healthier, your standards will naturally rise, and you won't be willing to settle for anything less than what you truly deserve.

Overall, the best approach is to stay single, become the person you want to marry, and maintain your high standards until someone who meets them and is genuinely interested in you comes along. It's better to be single and secure than to be in the wrong relationships. It's more lonely to be with the wrong people than to be secure by yourself. True happiness, confidence, and security doesn't come from a person. They come from knowing God, and remembering the truth about who you are in Him will set you free from needing other people's validation.

Body Image

I was searching for validation because I wasn't secure in myself, which led me to struggle with my body image more than I ever have. In today's generation, social media is a prevalent part of our everyday lives. With anything, social media has its advantages and its disadvantages. One of the disadvantages is the impact it has had on body image. I didn't have this experience with social media until I got to college. There, I was surrounded by people who cared what their profile looked like and how many likes they got on a photo. It was the first time I heard the term "Instagram worthy," meaning the photo or video had to be aesthetically pleasing in every way for it to be postable. There are levels to this, and if you are not careful it can be dangerous, affecting the way you see yourself.

There are a plethora of filters and editing apps today. These apps can change anything about yourself that you perceive as a flaw. You want better cheekbones? There is an app. You want a better figure? There is an app. You want fuller hair? There is an app. People are now able to magically fix what they view as imperfections on themselves at a swipe of a finger. This causes people to be so fixated on "perfection" that anything less means they aren't good enough. People go to the mirror, and when the reflection doesn't match the edited version of themselves, it causes their self-esteem to drop. They get on a Zoom call, and if the picture of them doesn't match the edited version of themselves, they are anxious about not looking good enough.

Eventually, I got caught up in trying to make my Instagram look perfect. The more I analyzed my photo, the more my "imperfections" were all I could see. The longer this went on, the more strict I became on what qualified as Instagram worthy. That just stole all the joy in sharing my memories with my friends on social media. I promise you, memories are way more enjoyable living in the moment than trying to capture the perfect picture.

Poor self-esteem or poor body image doesn't happen all at once. It's an accumulation of repeating the same negative thought to yourself over and over again until you believe it as truth. Sitting on your phone scrolling all day, comparing yourself to other people or a past version of yourself will just lead to being more and more unhappy with how you look. The eClinicalMedicine did a study and found the more time you spend on social media the more likely you are to be dissatisfied with your body and have poor self-esteem.[2] Additionally, certain environments you are in can contribute to poor body image if you are not guarding your thoughts. Some environments you have the power to change and some you don't, but you always have the power to guard your thoughts.

I really struggled with body image for the first time in college. I was living with people who said things like, "We need to drink apple cider vinegar to stay thin," or "Oh my gosh you know this cookie is 200+ calories? We would have to walk so many miles to burn that off, it's not even worth it." Hearing, "I only ate a bag of Skinny Pop today," was a normal occurrence. I didn't realize all of these conversations (amongst other things) were slowly influencing and feeding my poor thoughts about my body.

The next year, I saw a nutritionist and told her I liked to eat peanut butter jelly sandwiches as a quick on-the-go lunch. She told me that unless I have a heavy practice that day, I should only eat half of the sandwich. After that conversation plus my insecurity with my body already, I really struggled for a while with whether I deserved to eat normal meals if I didn't work out enough. Additionally, during preseason, we were required to weigh in and weigh out every morning to make sure we weren't losing too much water. I understand this is for our physical health, but starting each day by weighing yourself makes it difficult not to focus on the number on the scale. Not to mention, you see everybody else's weight; it's hard not to compare.

I got in the bad habit for a few months of standing in front of the mirror, staring at my body, as a cycle of phrases played on a loop in my mind. *You are fat. You shouldn't have eaten that last night. You need to skip your next meal. You don't deserve to have any sweets. You are not skinny enough.* I lost ten pounds during covid and became obsessed with staying at that weight or lower. I had terrible body dysmorphia. When I was at my lightest weight, I still thought I needed to lose weight, I was the most unhappy, and I didn't have any energy. This was not okay then, and it's not okay now. I don't have to earn the right to eat. I couldn't see it then, but as soon as I started eating normally, I realized everything before wasn't worth it.

The saddest part is, the beauty standard changes constantly. I was striving to reflect an image that isn't even reliable and is going to change. One day the goal was to be skinny, and the next day it was to be slim thick. How can this standard of beauty be true if it's constantly changing? It can't be. The truth is, God created man in His own image, and He will never change. Therefore, Jesus is the person we should aspire for our reflection to be, not this month's beauty standard.

Really, if you wouldn't speak to your best friend or your daughter the way you talk to yourself, why do you think you deserve to be treated like that? Your worth is not tied to a number on a scale or your appearance at all; it's tied to whose you are—child of God.

Even if you do get the "perfect body" or have the "perfect body," you are still not guaranteed to be happy with your reflection because you must adjust your mindset to fix your perception. This does not happen by accident. You have to intentionally decide to speak kindly to yourself even if you don't believe it. Instead of being your worst enemy, you need to become your biggest cheerleader. *I am beautifully and wonderfully made, God formed me so intentionally, I am accepted, I am enough, and I am loved.* Eventually, your mind will catch up to these truths. Once you know who you are in Christ, you begin wanting to take care of your body so you can do all that God has called you to do. Your self-care is not for vain reasons, but because it's a temple of the Holy Spirit and you want to steward the body God gave you well. I have found I always feel my best when I'm taking care of mind, body, *and* spirit. That means working out at least 30 minutes a day even if that just means a nice walk in the park and filling my mind and spirit with truth: God's Word.

It will always be easier to think negative thoughts because there is no opposition toward it. The enemy loves for you to agree with him. You must take ownership over your mind and begin to agree with what God says about you. The enemy fights so hard to keep you doubting yourself because he fears what you'll do when you begin to walk in the confidence God wants to give you. Your self-worth can only change if you start coming into agreement with the truth, His truth.

Banded Together

These things all banded together caused my self-worth to fluctuate. God showed me a vision of what I looked like in college. I was walking head high, shoulders back, with this bag over my shoulder, walking around like I deserved to be there. However, every time I perceived to have gotten rejected or I criticized my body, I added a rock in my bag. The bag kept getting heavier, but my appearance remained the same, until one day I added a rock, and the bag became too heavy. The bag instantly fell, forcing me to drag it. I couldn't just let the rocks out because I didn't know why I picked them up to begin with. Suddenly, I was walking with my head down, shoulders down, and leaning over, dragging the bag everywhere. The weight was heavy, and I couldn't see all that God had for me because my head was down. I got used to the rocks weighing me down. It was normal at that point. I didn't even remember what it was like not to have them.

After college, I felt like I hit rock bottom and knew there had to be something more. I didn't know it at the time, but that was the night I made the decision to get rid of the rocks. It was a journey because the only way you can get rid of the things weighing you down is to identify it and cast it to Jesus, then you will be set free. A freedom awaited me that I didn't even know existed.

By the end of my last semester, with soccer behind me, I felt more alone than ever. My closest friends had graduated, and all the unresolved rejections from the past were catching up to me. Six months later, I still harbored anger toward the mother of the guy I cared about deeply, as she was the reason we weren't together.

On top of that, I struggled with body image issues and was riddled by insecurity. Although I had many friends, nobody fully knew me—and worse, I didn't even know myself anymore. Layers of adapting to fit in buried what was truly me under what I had merely *chameleoned* into, and without soccer I didn't know where I belonged anymore.

It became clear that no matter how many people are around you, you'll always feel lonely if you don't allow others to truly know you or if you're pretending to be somebody you are not. I was well liked, but it didn't matter. My true desire was to be fully known and loved for who I am.

After I graduated, I was left with the aftermath of all my choices, and there's nothing worse than a bad aftertaste. Completing my last soccer season and earning my master's degree brought a brief sense of fulfillment, but soon after, the uncertainty of what lay ahead left me fearful. *Soccer has always defined my life; now*, I wondered, *what comes next?*

CHAPTER 4

DISCOVERING MY BROKENNESS

"One day, you are going to stand in front of the mirror and you are going to see yourself in Christ." —Crystal Sparks

After I graduated college, I had an identity crisis. I didn't know who I was, and I was so full of fear about my future. I was struggling to know where I fit into this world outside of soccer, while also needing to decide what career I would go into. I felt like my whole life was going to be set and determined by the job I chose. It felt like a make-it-or-break-it type situation. *What if I choose wrong? What if I don't have what it takes and I fail? What if I am in the wrong spaces, and I never get married because of it? What if I am miserable and I hate the profession I choose? What if my best days are behind me?*

The fear was paralyzing. I asked my parents what they thought I should do, and I went with their suggestion. At the time, I felt that if somebody could tell me what to do, it would take the pressure off of me. And if it didn't work out, it's really not my fault, but rather the person giving the advice. Later, I realized this isn't true. My life is my responsibility because whatever happens, I am the one who'll have to deal with the outcome, not them.

I had a month in between college and starting my new job. I had a hole in my heart from soccer and I was searching for anything to fulfill me. I resorted to the habits I developed in college. I was going to bars frequently to pass the time and enjoyed the attention from guys there. It temporarily made me feel better, but the feeling never lasted. I still had to go home alone and ponder what I was doing with my life. I found myself thinking, "Is this how it's always going to be?"

I knew I felt empty and lacked purpose, but I couldn't be honest about it. I couldn't even be honest with myself, let alone anybody else. I've always suppressed my emotions and defaulted to an "I don't care" exterior to protect myself. And this is something I've done for years. It felt like there was a dam holding back all of my emotions that I could feel trying to break, but I knew if I allowed it to, I would break into many pieces. *If it breaks, can I put myself back together?*

One night, I felt like I finally hit rock bottom. I prayed and asked God if He could help me. I didn't know what my purpose was. I didn't know if I was worth anything anymore because I didn't have anything to offer. That night I went to a bar, and a man approached me. In my head, I was already thinking, *This man wants something from me*, so my walls were up and I was standoffish. He said, "You don't look like you should be here; you look like you should be in church. You are too good for a place like this," and walked off. I can assure you, I did not have on a "church outfit." Immediately, there was a lump in my throat as I fought to hold back the emotions I buried. God met me right where I was.

I left the bar after that night feeling so seen for the first time in a long time and wanting to do better. The next morning at church, I felt like God was giving me the answer to all my fears. My pastor's message was based on Matthew 6:33 (NIV): "But seek first his kingdom and his righteousness, and all these things will be given to you as well." In other words, the Bible teaches to seek God first, and everything else will follow. The peace, guidance, security, love, hope, purpose, my identity, and divine relationships I desire all come from prioritizing God in my life first.

I wanted to listen to God, but no matter how hard I tried, I kept falling short and doing things I didn't want to do anymore. At the moment, it was fun, but afterward I'd feel guilty and be frustrated with myself. I'd question, *Why did you do that again, when you know you shouldn't?* I was discouraged, until my pastor pointed this scripture out from John 14:15 (NIV): "If you love me, you will keep my commandments." She said, "Some of you are living on the wrong side of the comma. You think you will keep God's commandments and then you'll love Him, but God is saying, 'Love Me and then you will keep My commandments.'"

I had the revelation that my obedience needed to be rooted in love rather than striving. I made a commitment that I was going to give God one year of my life. I would pursue Him with all my heart; no more one foot in and one foot out. If I don't feel any different in a year, then I'm done and I will continue to live however I want to. Honestly, I had nothing to lose and everything to gain.

I jumped right in by joining a Holy Spirit community group at my church. Essentially, the group offers you a new understanding of the Holy Spirit every week, including but not limited to spiritual gifts, your calling, past pain, spiritual warfare, and hearing God's voice. This was an eye-opening experience for me, as it began to uncover things I didn't realize were holding me back.

The room was filled with people I didn't know. We were learning the way God speaks and how to hear His voice. After the teaching, we did an exercise. They played soft worship music as we contemplated two questions: "My critic's name is…" and "My critic says…" We were to write the answers down in our workbooks that only we see. I've struggled with being a perfectionist and wanting to maintain an appearance that my life is perfect for as long as I can remember. Therefore, if we had to say our answers out loud,

I'd give a political answer or a general answer that didn't sound too bad instead of my real answer. Since it was just in our workbooks, I wrote the truth. It was the first time I slowed down long enough to acknowledge my inner thoughts.

After we finished, my pastor, the one who teaches the class, grabbed the microphone, called my name, and told me to come to the front. My heart dropped. Out of everybody in here, she chooses me?! I really don't mind being in front of people, but I did in this instance. As I was walking to the front, avoiding eye contact and staring at the floor, she invited another person up who is a prophet—someone who hears from God with great clarity. When this prophet prays for people, God often provides them with insight about that person's divine will or purpose.

My pastor asked the prophet to seek three words from God that He wants me to know. He responded that he felt like God wanted me to know I was Beloved, I am His Daughter, and he saw God putting a crown on my head to remind me I was accepted into His royal priesthood. My eyes immediately started to fill with tears because it directly contrasted with what I had written down about myself. Nobody knew what I wrote let alone what I felt, so for him to say exactly what I needed to hear wrecked me. Again, I felt so seen.

So, when my pastor asked if I'd be willing to share what I wrote, I decided to let my guard down a little. I grabbed the microphone shakily and began reading. "I am not enough," "I don't deserve to be loved," "If I am not the best, then I am a loser," "If you are not perfect then you failed," and "I talk too much." I honestly thought this of myself, and I couldn't believe God chose the words He did even after everything I've done. From the exercise, I realized I was my biggest critic, and I was determined to change this.

Throughout the group, I learned that your past pain plays a significant impact on how you live your life today and how you think about yourself. From the moment you are born, your brain is evolving. As you grow, your brain is making neural pathways. The more you think a thought, the easier it is for you to think that thought again. It's great if you have healthy thoughts, however, it is bad news if you don't. The lies we believe often originate from childhood experiences that repeatedly reinforced these falsehoods in our minds as we grew up until we eventually accepted them as truth. The great news is, you can expose the lies, change your thoughts, and create new neural pathways to agree with the truth about who you are. It says in Romans 12:2 (NLT), "Don't copy the behavior and customs of this world, but let God transform you into a new person by changing the way you think. Then you will learn to know God's will for you, which is good and pleasing and perfect."

I realized I'd been copying the world's viewpoint on where I placed my identity. I was looking to external things like sports, status, social media, boys, academics, or my career to tell me my worth and how I should view myself.

But none of these things created me. Even when I had everything I thought I wanted, I wasn't fully satisfied. God created us to need love, significance, and security, and I was just looking for it in the wrong places. So many voices bombard us every day with who we are not and the many ways we fall short. I needed to get plugged into the Source who says who I am and find out what He says about me. I needed to retrain my brain to know the truth, and that's what I did.

The Bible says God is always speaking to us, but I didn't know how to recognize His voice consistently, and I also had a misrepresentation of who God was. I began reading one chapter a day of the Gospel of John and wrote down God's characteristics that I saw in each chapter. Just like with any friend I meet, the more I spend time with them, the more I know their voice. Eventually, they can send me a text message, and when I read it, I read it in their voice because I am so familiar with it. The same is true with God. The more I spend time with Him by reading His Word and being in prayer, the more I'll know His character and be able to decipher what He is saying versus what the enemy is saying.

I struggled with this a lot at first because I still had so many voices speaking into my life and telling me who I was, what I was good at, and what I should do. There was too much noise; I couldn't hear God. At that point in my life, I valued my parents' opinion of me so much that I would've morphed unknowingly into whatever they told me I should do. However, doing this would just be falling back to the

59

mindset of *you are what you do*. I knew I wasn't at the point in my walk with God yet where I wanted to hear Him more than I wanted to please my parents, so I decided to set a boundary with my parents. I told them I valued their opinion more than anything, but I really wanted to find out who I am in Christ and discover my place in this world. So, I needed them to keep their opinions about me to themselves unless I specifically asked. They respected my boundaries, and it allowed me to have space to cultivate hearing God's voice for my life and develop my relationship with Him. The more I learned who He is, the more it helped me see who I am.

During this time, I also started going to counseling. I struggled to go at first for a couple of reasons. The first reason was I didn't think I had experienced anything in my life bad enough to warrant counseling. *Even though I want to heal my heart, do I even deserve to go? So many other people have had worse experiences than me.* I kept telling myself I should just get over my struggles. I always invalidated my feelings.

In time, I realized counseling is for everybody. You don't have to have a certain amount of hurt to go. The second reason is the negative stigma around therapy, and I didn't want people to think I was "crazy." Thankfully, I was more desperate to stop struggling mentally, so I decided to go anyway. I am beyond grateful that I did.

I made sure to pick a Christian counselor to ensure the person that I allowed to give me tools to walk me through my struggles and my pain aligns with my beliefs. I prayed before my sessions and asked God to lead the way and to give my counselor supernatural wisdom to speak into my life. After my sessions, I would sit with God and journal. Acknowledging my feelings, being honest about where I was at, and admitting my weaknesses were my first steps toward true strength and healing.

Through Holy Spirit Group, counseling, and sitting with God, the dam inside of me that was holding back my emotions broke; emotions I had held onto for years all came flooding out. I couldn't hold it together anymore, and the pieces of me shattered everywhere. I cried for months upon months. It was one of the hardest seasons of my life. I felt so out of control, and I didn't know how to process my emotions because I never validated them. The discomfort and pain overwhelmed me.

I wanted so desperately to hold onto something familiar to bring me comfort. I needed something to make me feel secure again, so I reached out to my ex-boyfriend, Tyler, who I had been on again and off again with. The reason we broke up was because of his mom. For a month I had been praying for God to help me forgive her because I was tired of carrying the anger. I knew the anger was just hiding the pain I felt from her words. So, I started praying for her as if she was my favorite person in the world.

At first my prayer was just to bless her. This was very challenging at first because I didn't want to bless her at all.

That's all I could manage. As I kept praying for her it got easier, and eventually God did something in me. He completely softened my heart to where I was truly able to forgive her. God let me see it from her perspective and gave me a compassion for her that only God could give. Since Tyler's mom and I were good, there was nothing keeping us from being together anymore. After all, he was the only man I dated that I thought I would marry one day.

I texted Tyler to see if he wanted to hang out. To my surprise, he told me he couldn't because he had a girlfriend. My jaw hit the ground. We both have talked to other people, but we never actually dated anybody else since we'd met three years prior. It felt like I got punched in the gut, so I responded with something along the lines of, "Fine, I'll date somebody else too." That was petty of me. I felt bad the next day and said, "Sorry, I am happy for you," but the truth is, I thought he should be with me. I figured she was a rebound and they'd break up soon. *I'll just wait it out.* But I brought it to God in prayer and said, "If this man is for me then bring him back into my life, and if he is not for me, make it clear because right now it feels like I lost the person who I was supposed to marry." I honestly thought I missed it.

My counselor had a different idea. She told me to make a choice for myself to close the door and lock it on this relationship, whether he was single or not. If this really was the person God has for me, I won't miss it. God will open the door. I had never grieved our break up before this because, again, I assumed we would get back together one day. Now,

I had no choice but to deal with these feelings. Talk about kicking someone when they're down.

A big part of me believed I was never going to get married and I only had myself to blame. In the back of my mind, I thought, *After I get healed, Tyler will want me back.* God would reopen the door.

I continued to work through my past pain in counseling and the walls around my heart started coming down. I really believed if Tyler and I had met then, after some healing, things would be different. I had so much love to give now. If he would just give me a chance, he would see I am worth it. I wanted to tell him, "I'm sorry I couldn't let you all the way in when we dated, but I'm better now. Just give me a chance." I was ready to fight for him and he shut me completely down.

At this point, I didn't care if we were dating or not, I just needed him in my life. *Can we be friends like we used to be?* I realized then that Tyler was my safety net. I was going to him to make me feel secure and comforted instead of sitting in discomfort with God. I knew I wouldn't hurt as bad if I had Tyler back in my life, but it's like putting a band-aid on a bullet wound. It doesn't heal the wound, it just covers it up. Eventually, he would let me down because a person was never supposed to fill God's place in my life. Looking back, I am so thankful God blessed Tyler with his person because I would've kept falling into the same pattern of going back to him and not dealing with the pain I needed to deal with. God was merciful though and He forced my hand.

There was nothing else I could do but surrender to God. I couldn't handle the heartbreak I was experiencing by myself on top of everything else. I wanted so badly to do something, but there was nothing more I could do. I had to lean on God in this season like never before. Needing answers, I prayed and asked God to tell me if Tyler is the one for me or not because I didn't know how to deal with the breakup and feeling like I missed it. God is so good. He gave me a dream one night, and in it, I knew Tyler was not for me. He is a great person, however He is not God's best for me.

In my dream, I was in a store with full-size Skittles and Starburst everywhere. I was sad because I didn't want candy; I wanted chocolate. Then, a few Milky Ways appeared scattered here and there. I thought, *These will do, I guess*, but it's not what I really wanted. As I kept walking, I found two individually wrapped gold Rolos hidden under the store. I was the happiest I've ever been because that was exactly what I wanted.

I prayed and asked God for the interpretation of my dream, and I felt like He told me this: There will be many men in the world I will not be interested in at all, represented by the Skittles and Starburst. Then, there will be a few men along the way, represented by the Milky Ways, that check enough of the boxes and would be good enough, but they are not the true desire of my heart. If I wait on

God's timing and do not rush ahead and settle, there is a man who is just for me—the true desire of my heart. We are hidden from each other now, but one day we'll find each other, and it'll be worth the wait. I won't have to force it or question if he is for me; I will know.

I felt so seen and loved by God. I still had the pain of wanting to be with this man, but now I had a word to stand on by God to silence the lies and remain hopeful.

It was truly just me and God in this season because, simultaneously, friendships started walking out of my life. At the time, it felt like just one more thing to add on. I was so hurt and felt even more alone. I now see God was shedding people out of my life who weren't contributing to the person He was building me up to be. I needed to distance myself from all the boy drama, the excessive drinking at the bars, the gossiping, and Instagram-worthy talks. I did not realize how much of an impact being in these environments and listening to these conversations were having on me until I wasn't in them anymore. I expected God to bring me new friends instantaneously, but that's not what happened.

I was still searching for my purpose and struggling with my confidence, so I got in rooms I knew would help me discover my calling. I got really plugged into my church and started going to a prayer prophetic group. This was a group of women who had cultivated hearing God's voice so well. They would always speak life over me and were instrumental in helping me learn to do the same. Being in spaces with people who are older and wiser exponentially grew my faith without me fully being aware of how much. It's like taking advantage of an opportunity for their ceiling to be my floor. I was a sponge when I was around these women, trying to soak up any wisdom they wanted to impart to me.

Then, I felt like God told me to enroll in One College, a ministry school. At first, I was like, *No thanks, I just got out of school and I do not want to go back.* I couldn't shake the desire to know more about what I believe and why I believed it biblically, but I didn't have anyone to help me understand the Bible. I imagine God just looking at me, eyes big, half smile, and nodding His head yes, like, *Duh that's the whole point of One College is to help disciple you, give you the tools to go deeper, understand the Word on your own, and accelerate your spiritual growth.* I committed to it without consulting anybody, which was a big step for me. This was the first decision I made just for myself—not to please anybody else.

CHAPTER 5

RELINQUISHING CONTROL

Every time I am driving, I put the address in my maps and put it on Apple CarPlay even if I know exactly how to get there. I like knowing my estimated time of arrival, and I don't want any surprises. Most of the time, my maps will detour me if there's going to be a delay for any reason, whether that be construction or an accident. I can see exactly why I have to go a back way or take an earlier exit, so I don't mind that the plan changed because I know it's taking me the best route to get to my destination. The best is when I beat my estimated time of arrival and arrive sooner than expected. That's grounds to give myself a pat on the back.

What I am really revealing is how knowing all the details brings me a sense of comfort and makes me feel a sense of control. It's not a big deal when it comes to driving; however, it becomes an issue when you won't give God the steering wheel of your life without knowing the whole plan. If God says to walk out of that relationship, accept a job that is below your current salary, move to a new city, have a season of singleness, or any other unexpected turn, would you do it even if you didn't understand why? God is not like the maps in terms of always giving you a reason why, but He is like the best version of the maps; He knows the quickest and best way to get you to where He wants to take you.

God is the Creator of the whole universe; don't you think He knows the best and quickest route to get you to where He wants to take you? The thing is, you'll have to trust Him, and this takes faith. Hebrews 11:1 (NKJV) says, "Now faith is the substance of things hoped for, the evidence of things not seen." It is clear in the Bible that it's impossible to please God without faith. If you follow His voice even when you don't understand why or it feels backward, you can trust God will get you to where He promised you right on time. Unfortunately, there is no beating the estimated time of arrival for God's timing. You can't force it when it's not God's timing. But praise God, when it *is* His timing, you can't stop it.

I was guilty of white knuckling my life's steering wheel when I went all in with the Lord. It was a process to learn to relinquish the control and trust that my life really is better in His hands than my own. I wish I could say the process of me handing over the reins to God was easy, but the truth is it was difficult and messy. Looking back, I can see it was also restorative and beautiful. I wouldn't trade the journey for anything because it was along the journey I got to know the Lord in a personal, intimate way.

Real change began happening after I graduated Sam Houston and I went all in with God. It was at the end of December 2021, and I kept hearing people talk about praying for a word for the year. The idea is to pray for God to give you a word to hold onto for that year and focus on. I didn't really know how to receive my word or what to expect. I just prayed and hoped I would recognize it when it came.

I prayed the entire month of December and felt like I heard nothing. By New Year's Eve, I still didn't have a word and felt like I had failed. *Maybe God doesn't speak to me in the same way He does to others.* The enemy often throws accusations at us, trying to make us believe something is wrong with us or that we haven't done something right. Deuteronomy 4:29 says, "But if from there you seek the Lord your God, you will find Him if you seek Him with all your heart and with all your soul." We have the assurance that if we seek God, we will find Him. Don't let your expectations of how it should look or the timeline you've set for yourself hinder you or make you believe the lie that you are falling behind or have failed. God's timing is perfect. As children of God, we do hear His voice. Don't allow the enemy to discourage you and make you give up prematurely. Keep seeking, and you will find Him as I did.

That day, I was on the phone with a friend, and every time she said the word "trust," it stood out to me. I felt a little nudge in my heart each time she said it. Ironically, I didn't trust that "trust" was actually my word. I didn't tell anyone about my suspicions. Instead, I prayed to God, asking if "trust" really was my word, to make it clear because, no offense...I didn't trust that it was.

A couple of hours later, my mom randomly sent me an article. Keep in mind, she didn't know I was even praying for a word for the year. The article was about a wealthy man taking a couple out to dinner. As they walked into the restaurant, the rich man saw a penny on the ground and picked it up. He smiled as he looked at what he had found. This man was not hurting for money and didn't need the penny. The couple's curiosity got the best of them, and they asked, "Why did you pick up the penny?" The man responded, "Because on the back of every penny, it says 'In God we trust.' I feel like God is dropping a message right in front of me, reminding me to trust Him. Every time I pass by a penny, it's an opportunity for me to stop and check if I am trusting God in my life. The penny is an invitation from God to start a conversation with me."

After reading this, I was convinced! My word for the year was definitely "trust." Plus, I never saw pennies the same way again.

I obviously had some trust issues. They stem from various experiences where people have let me down or betrayed my trust. The common denominator is that humans are imperfect. However, God is not human. The Bible says God is incapable of lying, so there is actually no one better to trust than God.

The problem was my need to feel in control. I knew I should trust God with my life, but I didn't. I trusted Him to be my Savior, but I struggled with letting Him be Lord over my life. I was terrified that I wouldn't get to where I wanted to be in life if I didn't make it happen myself. I thought I knew better and didn't understand why I needed to wait if I could just do it myself. Giving up control was a struggle because I felt safer believing I was in charge, even though I never truly was. This year was all about learning to give up control. Surrendering to whatever God wanted to do was the hardest lesson for me to learn, and it's a choice I still have to make daily.

Throughout the year, learning to trust God didn't happen all at once. As I mentioned it was a process, and I definitely stumbled from time to time, trying to manipulate situations, which made me see God's loving mercy on display even more. His kindness and goodness made me want to do things His way. I eventually prayed a bold prayer: *God, block anybody or anything that is not for me,* and He did.

As I started my first semester at One College, I was tired of feeling hurt, lacking the godly community I desired, and growing impatient. I asked myself, *Why are you feeling such a need to run ahead of God?* It was because I felt like I was falling behind again. Tyler had moved on, and I hadn't. It just didn't seem fair. I could see that God was calling me to a season of solitude, but I fought it tooth and nail. It was the opposite of what my heart desired. I didn't want it to just be God and me; I wanted companionship. I had allowed the fear that God couldn't do it or wouldn't do it for me to take over the driving seat.

In these moments, I wish I would have realized how much God loves me. First John 4:18 says, "There is no fear in love. But perfect love drives out fear." Meditating on God's love for you will begin to cast out the fear and doubt about whether He has good plans for your life. He is not leading you away from the promised land, but guiding you on a journey toward it. When God brought the Israelite's out of Egypt, away from bondage, they had to walk through the wilderness to reach the Promised Land. The wilderness didn't have everything the Israelite's wanted, but God always provided what they needed. It was never meant to be their final destination, only a necessary phase they had to pass through to get to the Promised Land. Similarly, when God delivers you from a situation, there is often a temporary season of pruning and refining where He prepares and leads you toward what He has in store for you.

You can trust wherever God is leading you is one step closer to your promised land even if it doesn't feel like it. He knows the steps to lead you to the most fulfilled life; however, you can't compare your journey to others' because their steps will look different from yours. The wilderness season is temporary, so don't prolong it by trying to get ahead of God. Lean into what He is trying to do in your life right now, and trust that while you are working on yourself, He is also working out every other detail of your life, including the people who are meant to be in it.

Unfortunately, my mind remained full of fear of my future, so I decided to "help" God out. I maintained that I was "surrendered" to God, but I thought I could make things easier for Him—as if the Creator of the universe needed my assistance. I began attending a large young-adults ministry called "The Porch" in Dallas every Tuesday night, even though it was an hour away from my home. My primary motive was to meet new people. In my mind, I believed there was no one in my hometown or church whom I wanted to be with, so I needed to go elsewhere.

With fear in the driving seat, you are more likely to make rash decisions out of desperation, which leads you to settling because *At least I got something or someone.* At this point, all I wanted was a godly man; nothing else mattered. Viewing things through this lens of desperation skewed my judgment, and I would have ended up settling for someone who is not God's best for me. I remember thinking I had met the cutest guy who loved the Lord, and I thought it was perfect. Hoping he would notice me, I walked past him, but he didn't approach me. So, once again, I took matters into my own hands and started a conversation with him. We exchanged texts for a few days, but it eventually fizzled out.

A couple of years later, I encountered him again at the same event. This time, I walked away with immense gratitude that God had blocked that relationship. With a healthier perspective, I could see clearly that we were not a match at all.

At the time, I really wanted to get married and felt pressured because my mom and sister both married at 20, and I was already 22. It may sound young, but being surrounded by early marriages made me feel behind schedule. I also believed that finding my life partner would solve all my insecurities and problems. Unable to meet new people due to my job being remote and knowing everyone at my church, I turned to social media. I tried a dating app before and decided it wasn't for me. I wanted to be more targeted with my search, so I looked on the Porch's Instagram and just followed random guys. I found someone cute and sent him a direct message—after all, you miss every shot you don't take, right? And you can always unsend a message on Instagram if they don't respond and pretend it never happened. That's what I did at least.

This man didn't reply, and I quickly unsent the message. It felt like rejection, but really it was just God's protection. There were things I needed to work through before I was ready to be in a healthy relationship. Even when guys did respond to me, I hesitated to meet them in person. It later dawned on me that I only engaged with emotionally unavailable men because I feared getting hurt again. This pattern of hurt people attracting hurt people led me into unintentional cycles of pain. In hindsight, I should have focused on personal growth with God instead of anxiously chasing my future and neglecting my present. By attempting to force my way out of the season God had placed me in, I unknowingly prolonged it and added unnecessary pain to deal with.

I didn't just look for connection with guys; I desired a godly group of friends as well. Similar mindset as before, it felt like when I got back from college everybody already had their friend groups, so I wasn't going to find it at my home church. Therefore, I went to a conference by myself at the young-adults church. I walked up to a random group of people that looked nice and asked if I could sit with them. They invited me to lunch later that day, and the whole conversation was about God and what we were going to take away from the conference. It was unlike anything I had ever been a part of—they were truly living set apart. I admired them so much and wanted friendships like theirs.

God had other plans, though. Out of all the people I could've gone up to, how did I choose the one group that was from another state? Although I never saw them again, I prayed that God would send me a friend group like that, one that would lead me closer to Him.

Feeling lonely still, I pivoted to my other comfort, soccer. I started playing in a co-ed league, which kept my schedule busy so I wouldn't have time to feel lonely. Although I was doing all the "right" things with God at this point, I didn't make time to sit with Him and address my feelings. I didn't realize I was avoiding those feelings by constantly filling my schedule. The fact is, you can know about God's healing, but until you make time to sit with Him, He can't heal what you don't acknowledge and bring to Him.

During this time, I began hanging out with a guy from the team whom I'll call Drew. Despite knowing we weren't aligned spiritually—he believed in God, but wasn't living his life for Him—I found myself falling into old habits.

Our initial texts were innocent and strictly friendly, until one night he kissed me. Then, I started riding with him to our soccer games out of convenience because he lived on the way. I would spend time with him before or after the games, kissing him as if we were together, even though I knew deep down I would never actually date him. The more I got to know Drew, the more it became clear that we didn't align on our viewpoints. Despite this, I started developing feelings anyway.

I was uncertain about how he felt about me, so when he went out to bars, I was tempted to want to join him strictly because I feared he would be with other girls if I didn't. These choices triggered feelings of comparison and self-doubt. Looking back, I should have ended our hangouts when I realized we didn't align on our values. My inner thoughts always told me to quit hanging out with him; however, I used our soccer games as an excuse to continue, and in the moment it was nice.

One day you're just staying over a little later because it is really not that big of a deal, and then you do it again and again because it really was fine. Then, somehow things escalate and you go too far, and you're questioning, *How did I get here?* At one point you knew you would NEVER cross *that* line, but somewhere along the way the line moved and you didn't even realize it. It's because little compromises lead to big compromises.

Thankfully, with Drew I maintained the boundary of waiting for marriage to have sex, but our situationship definitely pushed its limits, and I did find myself questioning, *How did I get here?* Drew never committed to me, even though he said he liked hanging out with me, I was his type, and acknowledged that his mom would actually want him to be with someone like me. Frustrated, I finally confronted him about why he didn't want a relationship. Deep down, I knew we weren't right for each other, but I struggled with conflicting feelings; I saw potential in him and hoped he would change if he cared enough about me. I know now, I can't change anybody. It's not how great I am or their love for me that will get someone to change; it's their love for God. He is the only One who can transform someone. I was at a crossroads, feeling convicted that continuing this situationship was not God's plan for me.

Ultimately, I had to decide: do I truly believe God's plan is better than mine? *My feelings are pulling me in one direction, but I sense that God is guiding me in another. My emotions feel so real right now, and it's hard to see beyond them.* This is the true test of trust. *Do I really believe God has good things in store for me, even when I can't see them? Do I truly trust that He knows better than I do and that His redirection is getting me back on track to a life that's better than I could ever imagine?*

My counselor told me to try journaling with God. At times, it feels like nobody understands what we are going through, but God does. Hebrews 4:15 (AMP) says, "For we do not have a High Priest who is unable to sympathize and understand our weaknesses and temptations, but One who has been tempted [knowing exactly how it feels to be human] in every respect as we are, yet without [committing any] sin." Jesus can sympathize with everything we are going through. He is not some far away God that can't be bothered. He is a personal God who weeps with us in the lows. Journaling with God is like having a written conversation with God. In order to be healed, you must identify what parts of you are broken. Journaling exactly how you feel helps you identify what you are truly struggling with so you can overcome it. It may manifest in our life as one thing, but it could stem from something else entirely. For example, I have a friend who recently got married. Every time they went somewhere, her husband was the first person to accept the offer to take leftovers home. Anger arose in my friend toward her husband every time this happened. It really didn't make sense why it made her mad, so she sat with the Lord about it. The Holy Spirit revealed to her the root was shame and it just manifested as anger. In her childhood, taking food home meant they didn't have enough, so now as an adult those unprocessed emotions are coming out in another way. The issue wasn't the food, it just triggered that feeling of shame. Now that she uncovered the root, she is able to sit with God and allow Him to heal that part of her and take home leftovers free from anger or shame!

By bringing your raw emotions, frustrations, and questions to God, you are telling Him how you feel. In return, He tells you what is true and heals the spaces you invite Him into. Our feelings are valid, but they are not reliable. They are constantly changing, but God's character remains constant. He is incapable of lying, so you can let go of the things He's asking you to and trust that He knows what's best for you. You can't see the full picture of your life, but He can. You can rest assured you will not be disappointed in the plans He has for you. As Matthew 7:11 (NIV) says, "If you, then, though you are evil, know how to give good gifts to your children, how much more will your Father in heaven give good gifts to those who ask him!" You can remain expectant in the anticipation of His goodness, knowing what He has for you is better than you could have ever imagined. It's worth the temporary discomfort of letting go of your plan to walk in the fulfillment of His promises for your life.

So, I committed to not seeing Drew again. I cut off all communication with him. Then, we would have a soccer game, I would see him, and we would hang out again. I'd leave frustrated with myself. *Ugh, why do I keep doing this?*

As I mentioned, I was enrolled at One College during this period. Throughout my Christian journey, I had often heard what we should believe and how we should live as Christians. However, I realized I was easily swayed because I lacked a firm foundation to explain why I believed these things. Attending One College helped me to deeply question my beliefs, understand why I held them, and learn how to support them with Scripture. The more knowledge I gained, the more I desired to align my life with God's teachings. Eventually, I felt so convicted by the influence of Drew, who was drawing me away from the person I aspired to be and from the presence of God. Again, I knew I had to make a decision and stick to it.

Being with Drew pulled me back into frequenting bars, stirred up insecurities, and slowly moved my boundaries. Despite my feelings for him and the fear of loneliness, I confronted a choice: indulge in sinful behavior or end this situationship. Mentally and physically, I couldn't sustain both paths. The peace and fulfillment I found in God's presence outweighed any temporary comforts. I knew I had to surrender this part of my life in order to align with God's calling for my life. I wrote in my journal.

Father God, I feel so alone and rejected. Two of my closest friends from college are no longer in my life. The last two guys I had feelings for walked out of my life. I know they aren't right for me, yet I keep checking to see if Tyler is still with his girlfriend, which frustrates me because I thought I was over him. I also keep seeking validation from Drew, even though I don't want to be with him. Honestly, the past few weeks, I am not even who I want to be. I'm tired of feeling alone and not feeling close to anybody. I have resorted back to my old sins and the way of living because I want to be a part of the group again. I'm afraid people won't like me because I have changed. I feel like sometimes I'm living two different lives—the one I want to live and the one that fits in.

I then felt like God told me this:

Ashley, you are feeling alone because I am going through a pruning process with you to make room for the things that I have for you. Take comfort that you are never alone. I am with you. Some people cannot come into the next season with you. You are still searching for man's approval to make you feel good enough, and it's causing you to compromise. I need to separate you for a season so you can see yourself the way I do and find what you have been looking for. I am the only one who will be able to fully satisfy your heart. Do not grow weary in doing good, for at the proper time you will reap a harvest, if you do not give up. My blood covers you, so do not dwell on the past few weeks. Just come back to Me and dwell in My presence and I will strengthen you. I want you to bring all your pain, frustrations, and struggles to me so that I can heal you and guide you. I am walking hand and hand with you. Listen to where I lead you and trust that I have good plans for your life. I am going to replace everything in your life with something better. Just rest in My presence and you'll be brought back to peace.

From my conversations with God, it was clear I needed a season of singleness to discover myself in Christ, not through relationships with boys. It was challenging because I enjoyed the attention from guys and having someone to call and text all day. I felt like I was going through withdrawals, looking at my phone multiple times a day, expecting there to be a text, and then remembering there wasn't going to be one.

I did really well not getting involved with any guy for a while, until I ran into Tyler's roommate. This unexpectedly stirred up all the unresolved feelings because Tyler had been out of sight and out of mind. Seeing his roommate brought everything rushing back. I did not want to feel those emotions, so I called Drew. I ended up going to his house and posting a picture on my Snapchat story showing I was with another guy.

Pride had crept in my heart, and I felt I had to prove that I had moved on and that other guys were interested in me too. The next day, I felt awful about going to Drew's house. I deleted the Snapchat post and apologized to God, realizing I should have turned to Him instead of seeking comfort and validation from Drew.

I stumbled, but my bounce-back timeframe was quicker this time. I immediately repented, so that was progress. I was embarrassed to admit that it bothered me. Logically, *I should be over Tyler by now.* I realized I'd been invalidating my feelings because I didn't feel entitled to them. My mind always went to, *You should be over it by now* or *It's not that bad.* I felt foolish for having feelings and believed I just needed to move on. Deep down, I knew I shouldn't be with him, so feeling conflicted made me feel even worse. I realized time doesn't heal all wounds if you never truly face your feelings. The problem was I was trying to apply logic when it wasn't my mind that was broken—it was my heart. So, rather than leaning on logic, I needed to learn to be kinder to myself and allow myself to feel whatever I needed so I could truly heal. Feel it, and He can heal it.

However you feel is okay. It doesn't matter how long it's been. It doesn't even have to make sense. Don't beat yourself up for having normal human emotions. Start acknowledging how you feel and allow God to heal those parts of you and remind you of what is true. There are layers to healing, so even when something triggers old feelings, it doesn't mean you're backsliding—it means God is working on healing another layer. Be kind to yourself; you are doing better than you think you are.

Unfortunately, my mind was consumed with doubts and really questioning if I heard God right about having a spouse for me, so that took priority over dealing with my feelings. This fear was paralyzing because it's a dream of mine to be a wife and mom one day. I worried about all the details: where, when, who, and how. The uncertainty made me grow increasingly impatient. I was so tempted to force it or look behind me. At least, I knew what I was getting with Tyler. Sure, we weren't perfect, but I knew we could be happy. At the time, I didn't realize what I would have been forfeiting if I went back to something God delivered me out of. I begged God to confirm that He does have someone for me so that I knew I didn't miss it or mess it up.

God never ceases to amaze me. He is so patient and gracious with us. He won't dismiss us or make us feel terrible for having doubts. He will meet us in our doubts and ease our minds, and that's what He did for me. I attended a conference and a prophet gave me a word from God about my husband: "Sometimes in the natural you want to get impatient, but it's really important that in this season, you allow this process to develop in you, because through the process, He is preparing you and making you ready. There is great value in the covenant and connection that He will bring to you, but He wants for each of you to be whole in and of your own selves. He wants each of you to have a key to the piece of the puzzle so that when you get together, it will be so bright and big and powerful. I see each of you carrying a piece of His light, glory, and heart, and when you are together and you connect those pieces, it will be explosive—the growth and the good thing that God produces in you and through you, in your marriage and through your marriage. So, do not get impatient. Don't listen to the lies that you missed it or you messed it up because it is not true. You are in His perfect timing."

Goodness, there is nothing like a word from God that can renew hope in an instant and build your faith! It brought me peace beyond measure and confirmed that I really *did* hear God correctly about my dream. I've found it's much easier to be patient and trust God when I truly believe He has this good future in store for me. I have been able to stand on this word every time the enemy comes back and tries to convince me otherwise.

I decided that no matter what I feel like doing, I'm not going back to past relationships because nothing is too costly for me to lay down in order to be obedient and walk in God's will for my life. I've learned that if God is calling me out of any relationship, it's because the relationship will cause damage, so it's for my own benefit to obey.

God will never call you out of a relationship because He doesn't want you to be happy. He knows something you don't, and He is trying to protect you. You don't want to forfeit the incredible future God has planned for you just because you won't let go of what's not meant for you. Will you choose to sacrifice temporary desires now for the greater fulfillment and joy that God has in store for you? The decision to trust Him will lead you to the life you truly desire.

Although I know it's in my best interest to let go, I am not strong enough to let go on my own; I need God's help. I confessed to God how much I was struggling. Finally, I let God in the driver seat. I truly surrendered to whatever He wanted me to do and invited Him into my pain.

God reminded me of how I always felt like something was missing with Tyler from the very beginning, and I had to convince myself otherwise. It really didn't make sense for something to be missing because he had everything I thought I wanted, so I thought it was because of my own walls and resorted to blaming myself. Now, I realize that God was telling me all along that we were never meant to be together. I didn't fully understand God's voice, so I dismissed His guidance and rationalized why I should be with him. If I had listened, it would have saved me and Tyler a lot of hurt.

The lies the enemy kept telling me were, *I missed it because of his mom, I missed it because the timing wasn't right and I wasn't healed,* or *It's not going to get any better than this and I missed it.* By sitting with God, I was reminded of the truth: we were never meant to be together. It's not about me not being good enough or him not being good enough. It's not because of his mom or the timing. It's simply because we are not God's best for each other. God was redirecting us, for our own good, to the people who are meant for us to fulfill the calling and purpose in our life. The man God has for me will come with peace, and He is preparing us both for each other. If I could feel this way with the wrong guy, imagine how great it would be with the right guy.

This revelation gave me so much freedom because I could silence the accuser, the enemy, from making me feel like a horrible person who ruined God's plan for my life. The fact is, God is bigger than we are. When you maintain a heart of surrender and repentance, God has a way of getting you back on track, no matter how many times you have messed up or how far you have strayed.

The greatest thing I can do is seek God and continue to allow Him to transform me from the inside out and trust that He really does have good plans for my life. Exposing these lies allowed me to let go of the last thing tying me to Tyler. I was finally able to shut the door in my heart to him, not just because I needed to, but because I was ready.

I see now it was a blessing. Although 2022 was filled with a lot of people being taken out of my life, what I gained was so much more. Having this time with just God and I helped me discover Him in a whole new way. I'd never felt Him so near before. My heart was hurting, but God comforted me in a way I'd never experienced before. I experienced His love in a new, deep way. In these moments when all hopes seemed lost, God told me, "I've got you." I felt like I was hanging off a cliff, with Jesus kneeling over, holding my hand. I was dead weight, and He was the only thing keeping me from falling. It made me realize that I can't do this without God, and He was not going to let me go.

I learned to trust that God knows better than I do and He always has a purpose for a waiting season. I really believed I was ready to get married, but now I see I was nowhere near ready. As I spent time with God, I discovered that I not only needed to find my identity in Him, but also work through certain issues with Him before I could have a healthy relationship. God needed to develop certain qualities in me and help me find who I truly was at my core.

Speaking of who I am at my core, there were a couple messages I needed to overcome that I may have misinterpreted as a young girl. Growing up, my dad always told me I didn't need a man, that I was an independent, strong woman, and that I didn't need to change my last name—they could change theirs. He even said I didn't want to hold boys' hands or kiss them. He was well-meaning in this, just doing what dads do, but because I valued his opinion so much, I felt I had to be this way to make him proud. This is far from the truth; my dad would be proud of me no matter what, but as a little girl, that's how I interpreted it, and it became a stronghold in my life. My dad bragged about his strong independent daughter who isn't worried about boys to his friends, which only reinforced my belief. It's great to be a strong independent woman, however, I took it to the extreme of believing I shouldn't need anybody in general. It made it difficult for me to ask for help outside of my family.

Additionally, I never saw my parents being affectionate toward each other growing up. My mom is just not an affectionate person. I grew up always hearing how Hallmark movies and cheesy messages were lame, which made me feel like there was something wrong with me for loving the cheesy stuff. I pushed this part of my personality down because I didn't want to be judged. She always made comments about my dad for being mushy, so I assumed that it was bad.

When I got a boyfriend, I felt uncomfortable showing affection in front of anyone I knew, especially my parents. I didn't want him to hold my hand or cuddle with me when people were around. I would sit on one end of the couch and I wanted him to sit on the other. Even though I liked him and wanted to be with him, it felt like I was doing something wrong. It seriously made me anxious that people were watching me. I thought I was just someone who didn't like physical touch. When I went to college, I realized that wasn't true. I just feared disappointing my dad and wanted to please him.

I didn't want to take my future husband's last name because *Why did I have to be the one to lose my identity?* I was so adamant about this, but I couldn't explain why. God revealed to me I just adopted what my dad said growing up as my own belief. God completely transformed my perspective and softened my heart toward a relationship. Now, I truly think it is an honor to take my future husband's last name. I want to be his biggest cheerleader, honor, and respect him. I will be proud to show him off to the world because I am so lucky God chose me to be his wife.

Now, I've learned how to be in tune with my emotions and communicate effectively. I learned how to love myself and to love God, so now I can properly love him and other people. And when it comes to being fiercely independent, I've learned we were created to need people in our life, so it's actually good for me not to try and do everything on my own.

All this time, I thought I was being rejected by these guys, but God was just trying to protect me. He knew I wasn't ready, and He was shielding me from potentially being hurt worse. When I stepped back and realized this wasn't happening *to* me but *for* me, my whole perspective shifted. Instead of feeling rejected, I felt loved. God loves me so much that He was protecting and redirecting me all along. My heart shifted back to gratitude.

He proves time and time again that our lives are better in His hands than in our own. People cannot control the outcome, but God can.

Luke 5:4–6, 8, 11 (NIV) says, "When he had finished speaking, he said to Simon, 'Put out into deep water, and let down the nets for a catch.' Simon answered, 'Master, we've worked hard all night and haven't caught anything. But because you say so, I will let down the nets.' When they had done so, they caught such a large number of fish that their nets began to break. When Simon Peter saw this, he fell at Jesus' knees and said, 'Go away from me, Lord; I am a sinful man!' So they pulled their boats up on shore, left everything and followed him."

Simon had no luck catching any fish all night, and as a seasoned fisherman, he knew exactly what he was doing. Jesus told him to let down his net again. Keep in mind, he had just fished all night and came up empty-handed. It didn't look promising, but he obeyed anyway. In an instant, Jesus provided not one fish, but an abundance of fish. Simon's response was to fall at Jesus' knees, leave everything, and follow Him because he experienced a taste of what life would be like surrendered to God's plan for his life.

Originally, Simon had the illusion that he was in control. He chose the boat, the time to fish, and the net he used, yet he couldn't control the outcome. He didn't set out intending to catch nothing, yet that's exactly what happened. Sometimes life feels this way. You have worked extremely hard, poured everything into a business, career, or relationship, yet you have nothing to show for it. The outcome you desired is not panning out, and now it feels hopeless.

I want to remind you that you will never fail when your hope is in Jesus. When you surrender control and trust in His plan, you can be assured that if it's not good, God's not done. He will work everything together for good. In an instant, Jesus can change everything. His timing is perfect.

What Simon couldn't do all night, Jesus did in seconds; where there was lack, God provided an abundance.

God wants to do the same in your life if you will let Him. If you listen to His voice and obey, it will lead you to a life of fulfillment and abundance. He knows exactly which business you should start, the right school you should attend, the right spouse for you, and the ideal business partner. He knows precisely what you need. The question is, will you trust Him?

It's important to understand that God sees the future and knows the best path to get you where you need to go. Unlike us, He isn't limited in power, knowledge, or resources. You can't force things when it's not God's timing, but when it is, nothing can stop it. Surrendering to and trusting in God's plan takes the pressure off you. You no longer have to worry about how it will happen; you can have peace knowing that God will make it happen. You can have complete confidence that whatever God has promised you will come to pass.

The only way to know what God has promised you is to create space to hear His voice. Set aside quiet time and make a dedicated space for Him to speak to you. For me, God is always faithful to meet me during my runs. Maybe for you, it's on your way to school, work, or even in the shower. Find whatever works best for you, away from distractions.

Once you've created that space, you need to believe that you *can* hear His voice. Jesus in John 10:27 (NKJV) says, "My sheep hear my voice, and I know them, and they follow me."

As a child of God, you are wired to hear His voice. The more you spend time with Him, the easier it will be to recognize it.

Next, you need to believe what God says is true. As Numbers 23:19 (NIV) says, "God is not human, that he should lie, not a human being, that he should change his mind. Does he speak and then not act? Does he promise and not fulfill?" Whatever God has promised you is a done deal, and He's not going to change His mind. It's not a matter of if, but when. You can rest knowing that God is working out every single detail to ensure your promise is in your path.

Having experienced God's goodness and faithfulness in my own life, my response mirrors Simon Peter's posture of surrender. I simply want to follow where God is leading. Reflecting on the hard times and seeing how God always showed up reminds me of His goodness and faithfulness. My natural response to such experiences is gratitude and in response, I felt compelled to repent and thank God.

Father, I thank you for who You are. I exalt Your name. You are all knowing and all powerful. You know best and nothing limits you. My life is better in Your hands than in my own. I'm sorry for thinking I knew better. I am sorry for the times I doubted and questioned You. I'm sorry for trying to run ahead of You and forcing my plan. I hand my future back into Your hands. Thank you, Jesus, for blocking me from settling for less than Your best. Thank you, Jesus, that even when I was crying on the bathroom floor begging You to restore my relationship, You didn't. Thank you for saying no to the wrong people so I didn't miss the right one. Thank you for not giving me my future husband prematurely. I know it hurts You to see me in pain, but You love me too much to give me something that is not for me or I am not ready for. Thank you for giving me the time to heal and for opening my eyes to the truth. Thank you for being patient with me and giving me grace. I pray You help me to align with Your perfect timing. Help me to be patient. I pray You continue to prepare me to be a good wife and for the purposes that You have in my life. Thank you in advance for the spouse You have for me and the plans You have for my life. I can trust You always fulfill Your promises and exceed expectations so I can rest, knowing this matter is sealed, in Jesus' name, amen.

Looking back, I am in awe of how much God loves me. He gave me the strength to not go back to something He delivered me out of in a time of weakness. He empowered me to sit in discomfort because He knew what was on the other side of it: healing. God picked up every piece of me, one by one, and put me back together. If I had continued to go back to my old safety nets, I wouldn't have sat long enough to allow God to heal me. It's mind blowing how much I would have forfeited in my life if I didn't let go of the things and people God told me to. The blessing is always on the other side of my obedience.

I needed this season of "trust" to find my identity and worth, to discover my purpose, and to grow my connection with the only One who can fully satisfy my heart. I always heard people say you can only be fully satisfied in Christ, but I didn't really believe it because I had never experienced it. By the end of that year, I can say that for the first time, my heart was full and I was completely satisfied in Christ alone. There are still things to work through and there will be ups and downs in my journey, but I now have my hope in someone who will never let me down.

The more I discover who God is, the easier it is to relinquish control and trust Him. God wants to reveal Himself to you in new ways, expose the lies that hinder you, and help you to step into the fullness of who He created you to be. He's just waiting on you. He made the first move by sending His Son to die on the cross, giving us a bridge to Him. Now, the ball is in your court. Will you respond and draw near to God?

CHAPTER 6

DISCOVERING GOD THROUGH THE CORRECT LENS

The more time I spent with Jesus and experienced His love and kindness, the more I desired to do better. I was trying to follow God's will for my life, and I hated that I still wanted to do things that I knew weren't good for me. It was like my heart was in a constant tug-of-war. Do I say no to God or to the club that's calling my name? Do I say no to God or to the boy that's no good for me, but makes me feel less lonely? Do I say no to God or to the friends I've known for years—the ones He told me can't come with me in my next season? My spirit won the tug of war most days, but I wasn't perfect. Desperately wanting to be perfect, I was extremely hard on myself. Now that I had been immersed in God's presence and was finding myself in Him, I wanted to please Him and be the perfect daughter. There were days I was confident God had favor for me, and there were days I struggled with feeling like *I've lost God's favor in my life because I'm not good enough.* If I didn't do enough that day or that week; I figured I had messed up one too many times.

I felt like such a horrible person for the choices I had made in my past. Why do I have all these desires I am fighting not to give into? I wanted to know every rule so I could make sure I was doing everything right. It felt like walking on a tightrope with no room for error. Being perfect at all times is necessary to walk with Jesus, right? I thought so, but what I failed to realize is God has grace for me and He's going to guide me well. He's not going to let me fall. I needed to quit thinking if I didn't hit this incredibly high standard then I'd never reach my full potential. It felt like one wrong move would disqualify me from what God had for me and then I wouldn't be good enough to be used by Him.

One day, my pastor, Pastor Crystal, approached me and said she felt like God showed her a vision of me and gave me the interpretation. She said, "There was an award ceremony happening, and you were out in the audience and there was somebody in third place and second place. And the Lord, through the Holy Spirit, was beckoning you to come, that you have a place. You see everybody else as further along than you, better than you, or has accomplished more than you. You keep beating yourself down like, 'I am this old and I have only done this…' and the Lord is like, 'Really?' You are doing so good and you are doing so much better than you think you are. And you see yourself as a person in the audience, but actually there is a place for you, and He wants to honor you and celebrate what a good job you have done and how far you have come and how much you have accomplished, but more than anything for who you are."

For God to tell me there was a place for me in spite of everything I've done meant everything. What I failed to see is that I don't have to be perfect to be valued. I don't have to have all the answers or have it all together all the time to be doing a good job. I don't have to be as far along as somebody else to be celebrated. I needed to start acknowledging and celebrating the small victories in my journey and quit comparing myself to everyone. I needed to quit discrediting all the progress I made when I would stumble. God gives me grace to cover every mistake, allowing me to keep moving forward rather than feeling like I'm starting back at square one. God showed me that when a caterpillar turns into a butterfly, no matter what it does, it can't turn back into a caterpillar. In the same way, when I became a child of God, no matter how many times I mess up, I can't lose my place in His Kingdom nor can I lose God's love.

In one of my counseling sessions, I discovered I had a wrong belief: I had to earn love. We went back to my childhood to find where this lie began and took root. One of the memories I was taken back to was when I was a little girl and had just won 4th place at the 3v3 World Championship Soccer Tournament in Orlando, Florida. *Fourth place?* I was so disappointed in myself. When we left the hotel to fly home, I left the trophy on the bed because I didn't think I deserved one.

As I sat in this memory, my counselor told me to picture Jesus there with me and to show Him the trophy. I didn't want anybody to see my 4th place trophy because it wasn't good enough, but I showed Him anyway. I could see Jesus smiling at me as if He was the most proud of me He's ever been. He still loved me even though I wasn't the best. At that moment, Jesus just hugged me.

I finished my session and sat in the new revelation that I didn't have to earn God's love. I turned on a random worship playlist on shuffle. The first song that came on was "Jireh" by Maverick City. The music was quiet, but the lyrics were so loud to me at that moment. The song speaks of how we'll never be more loved by Him than we are right now. It even mentions not needing a trophy to make Him proud.

Immediately, I broke down, overwhelmed by God's love and goodness. I felt such a weight lift, which reiterated and confirmed the revelation I received during my session. I realized I had a misrepresentation of who God is, and it was impacting everything I did. This revelation set me free. I am not perfect, and I don't have to be! Over the years, I have learned to never accept anything but the best. It's one thing to not settle, but it's another to be so hard on yourself that anything less than perfection is not good enough.

I grew up watching my dad, who was also my coach, throw away some of his coaches' trophies that were less than first place. As an adult, I know my dad has always been my biggest fan and has always been proud of me. However, as a little girl, it felt like I was disappointing him. That's when I started copying my dad. When I threw my trophy away, I was reiterating the lie to my subconscious that *if you're not perfect, you're not enough.* Of course, that is far from the truth, but it's what I believed. This lie overflowed into every area of my life: relationships, work, sports, everything. If someone came up to me and said, "You did amazing in the game," my first thought was always a rebuttal. "Did you not see my mistakes?" Even if it was just one. They saw everything I did right, but I could only see the one thing I messed up. I had programmed my mind to believe a lie for so long that if I didn't have it all together, I didn't deserve to be complimented or praised. Even when I replied, "Thank you," I secretly believed I was a phony, thinking, *If only they knew I wasn't actually perfect.*

One day, someone asked me, "When was the last time you extended grace to yourself?" The standard I had set was unattainable, and I would always fall short. No matter how much I strive in life, I'll never be good enough if this is the standard. But there's great news: it's not the standard. It's actually not about me at all. It's about who Jesus is and what He did for me. When I understand this, I am set free from striving and the need to be perfect. Grace covers all my shortcomings, and it is enough. I just have to receive it. But how?

First, I needed to shift my thoughts. I needed to make sure I was living from God's approval, rather than seeking people's approval. God already accepts me. When God spoke to me through the lyrics about not needing a trophy to make Him proud, He was reminding me that it's not about what I do that makes God approve of me or want a relationship with me. So why is it so important for me to continuously achieve the next goal or have it all together? What am I afraid will happen if people see I have vulnerabilities? Do I think people will think less of me if they see that I don't have it all together? Will my imperfections or moments of weakness expose me in a way that makes the ones I love, love me less?

Logically, the answer is no, but buried deep inside, I believed that lie to be true. God spoke to me again and said, "You will never be more loved than you are right now." God loves me unconditionally right now. He's not waiting for me to become a better person to finally love me. He's not waiting for me to clean up my act so He can finally love me. He's not waiting for me to be the best at everything so He can finally love me. He is not waiting on me at all to love me.

He proved His unconditional love for me that while I was still a sinner, He sent His only Son to endure a brutal death so that I can have a relationship with Him. There is no greater act of love than this. It's a love I cannot earn; I just have to receive it.

Father, You are worthy of all my praise. I thank you for who You are. I thank you that even when I rejected You, even when I chose other things or people over You, You still chose me. Father, You are omnipresent, so there is nowhere I can flee from Your presence. Thank you that when I was blackout drunk, You loved me in those moments just as much as you love me at church on my knees worshiping You. I thank you for loving me right where I am and for extending me grace. Father, I pray You help me to receive Your love and Your grace more fully, in Jesus' name, amen.

As I got into community groups at my church, I realized I wasn't the only one who had a past or faced struggles. I was genuinely shocked that the people I saw as "super Christians" weren't perfect. It made me feel so much better —not because I wanted them to have a past, but because I realized I had been comparing my worst moments to the best versions of themselves. Slowly, I began to see that I am not defined by my past. It took me a while to fully grasp this because I still kept certain things hidden.

The times when I did share what I was struggling with, the people in my group had already walked through similar challenges. This made me feel validated because I wasn't alone, and not only that, but they had the key I needed to unlock my healing. They were able to offer me wisdom and pray for me to experience the same freedom and victories they had experienced. Revelation 12:11 (NIV) says, "They triumphed over him by the blood of the Lamb and by the word of their testimony."

What God does for one person, He can do for another. As I listen to what God has done in their lives, my faith grows. Simply by being in these rooms, my expectations were being raised. The dreams that once were dormant because they seemed impossible began to wake up. Suddenly, the God I knew was becoming a lot bigger. Not only was I starting to see God's expectations of me were different than I initially thought, but my eyes were also opening to who God really is.

I was thinking so small before. *God can do what?!* He can literally do anything. He has no limits. It makes me think of when I am on an airplane, looking out the window high in the sky. Everything looks so tiny. The closer we get to landing, the bigger everything appears. My problems may seem big to me because I'm so close to them; however, God's view is even higher than the plane, so everything is truly tiny to Him. God is not limited. Anything I am dealing with is small compared to how big God is.

For example, I was praying for God to help my dad with the pain he's experiencing in his body. The doctor said they can't do anything to help, so in my mind, any relief would be amazing. Then, I was in the room when someone was telling their testimony—I'll call her Sarah. She said her brother was in a horrible accident. When she got to the hospital, everybody looked so defeated. He was connected to all sorts of machines and wasn't looking good.

Sarah knows God. Like…really knows God. She went into the room like she knew something different than everybody else. She prayed and declared complete healing over her brother. She didn't agree with what the doctor's report said or how it looked. She agreed with what the Word of God says, and God did a miracle. Her brother is alive and well, and you'd never know by looking at him that he had that accident. Her experience built my faith to believe and declare complete healing in Jesus' name over my dad— nothing missing, nothing broken. I don't care what it looks like, and it doesn't matter what the doctor says. My God is in the healing business, and I choose to agree with what He says, not the enemy.

The more I learned about God, the more I realized I did not really know Him before. I knew various things about God, but I didn't understand His true character. It's important to know the truth about who God is because our view of God will affect how we live and how we see ourselves. In my experience, there are a few different mindsets people tend to have about God.

Works-Based Mindset

My distorted viewpoint of God was that I had to earn His love and salvation. If I didn't do everything right, I thought I disqualified myself for what He had for me.

A friend asked me once how sure I was that I'm going to heaven on a scale from one to ten. I answered, "Maybe six or seven." She told me the only correct answers are zero or ten. The Bible says in Ephesians 2:8–9 (NIV), "For it is by grace you have been saved, through faith—and this is not from yourselves, it is the gift of God— not by works, so that no one can boast." Therefore, truth says nothing I ever do can earn me my salvation. It's a free gift from God; I just have to receive it by faith in Jesus. I can have 100% assurance that I am saved. If I didn't do anything to earn my way in, then nothing I do can earn my way out either.

God knew the enemy would try to convince His children that His love was conditional on what we did. The enemy knows that the moment we realize how much God loves us, all fear is cast out and our confidence in the plans God has for us increases. Saving us was proof enough that God loves us, but He wanted to reiterate it to ensure we know that nothing can ever separate us from His love.

Romans 8:38–39 (ESV) says, "For I am sure that neither death nor life, nor angels nor rulers, nor things present nor things to come, nor powers, nor height nor depth, nor anything else in all creation, will be able to separate us from the love of God in Christ Jesus our Lord." God has listed out every possible attack the enemy might use against us and disarmed them all. There is nothing I have done or will do, no being or place, not even death, that can separate me from the love of Christ. God loves me, period.

Police Officer Mindset

For some, their distorted view of God is that He's like a police officer, enforcing rules to prevent anyone from having fun. The truth is, God doesn't give us commandments and convictions to restrict our enjoyment, but to protect us and guide us toward a fulfilling life.

Imagine driving on a highway with guardrails on both sides. These guardrails aren't there to limit you; they keep you safe. Without them, people could get seriously injured if they veered off course. This analogy reflects how God cares for us. He provides guardrails in our lives through Scripture and the Holy Spirit. When we heed His guidance, it leads to life, peace, and contentment. The Bible says in John 10:10 (NKJV), "The thief does not come except to steal, and to kill, and to destroy. I have come that they may have life, and that they may have it more abundantly."

If we choose not to listen to God, we risk going down the path the enemy wants for us and facing the consequences of ignoring God's protection. I fell into this in college. If I had listened to my convictions about not getting drunk and not kissing boys I shouldn't have been with, I would have saved myself a lot of hurt and preserved my self-worth. God only tells you to remove something or someone from your life because He knows it will cause damage. The longer you hold on, the more damage it can cause.

When God told me to let go of Drew, I knew I should, but I didn't want to because it was fun and exciting. It felt like I blinked, and I was dragged back into a lifestyle and mindset I was working hard to escape. There were little compromises here and there that seemed insignificant, yet made a big impact over time. I found myself questioning my worth, facing lust temptations, and feeling further from God all over again. In hindsight, did the moments of excitement and fun outweigh the inner turmoil? No. It's never worth it.

Satan, the enemy, seeks to ruin our lives. He presents enticing offers and pleasures, but then condemns us afterward. When it comes to temptations, it's the enemy's strategy to entice us to do it, and once we do, condemn us for being a *horrible person*. Can we just get off his merry-go-round of insanity?

Satan always over-promises and under-delivers. God, on the other hand, promises good things and exceeds our expectations. When God says *no*, it's for our best interest, not to withhold anything good from us. His way is always better in the end.

God Is Love Mindset

Some people believe that because God is love, He isn't concerned with their sins as long as they're generally good to others. This mindset suggests, "I can live however I want as long as I treat people right." While God is indeed loving, He is also holy.

When you accept Jesus as your Lord and Savior, all your sins are forgiven, you are reconciled to God, and you receive a new heart. It says in Ezekiel 36:26 (NIV), "I will give you a new heart and put a new spirit in you; I will remove from you your heart of stone and give you a heart of flesh." Our new heart desires to live a life of holiness, and therefore you'll want to change to become more like Jesus. God will start convicting you of things that are not aligned with His will for your life. Conviction is a feeling or knowing in your conscience informing you of the things you should or shouldn't be doing. It should lead a Christian toward repentance and ultimately to spiritual growth and a better life in God's will. It's not that you *have to* change, it's that you'll *want to* change because of your love for Jesus.

As Christians, we all have the same commandments to follow in the Bible, but we also have personal convictions. Dr. Tony Evans explained it well: "In football, every team has to follow a specific rule book, but each team has its own playbook. The same is true for Christians. Every Christian has the same commandments to follow, but each will have certain personal convictions that not everyone else will have."

For example, I can't watch certain movies, but not every Christian shares that conviction. Some people feel convicted about listening to secular music, but I do not. Personal conviction only becomes a sin when God convicts you of something, and you continue doing it.

Unfortunately, our flesh and spirit are in direct conflict with each other, and our flesh still pulls us toward sin. This internal struggle often feels like an ongoing battle over how we should live. It's why I felt like my heart was in a game of tug-of-war. Until we choose to deny our flesh and commit to living a life of holiness, we won't experience inner peace.

Romans 8:6 (NIV) says, "The mind governed by the flesh is death, but the mind governed by the Spirit is life and peace." Whatever you choose to feed—whether your flesh or your spirit—will grow stronger. If you do things like live however you want, chase fame, money, or sleep around to try and fulfill yourself, you are going to be disappointed. Some of the most famous, richest people in the world are the most *unhappy*. Why? It's because they are not chasing after the One who they actually need.

Philippians 3:8 (NIV) says, "What is more, I consider everything a loss because of the surpassing worth of knowing Christ Jesus my Lord, for whose sake I have lost all things. I consider them garbage, that I may gain Christ." Paul is clear that nothing can compare to what one gains in Christ. I've personally experienced the fact that just one day in God's presence surpasses the value of 99 days without Him, and I've learned that nothing is too costly to give up in order to remain in God's will for my life. Feeling separated from God for even a moment by my sin is the worst feeling ever. I don't want anything to hinder my relationship with the Lord, so I continuously pray for God to remove anything or anyone from my life that would hinder our relationship. Over time, I realized I can live without the things God has promised me, but I cannot live without God. I would rather be in the valley with God than on the mountaintop with everything I ever wanted without God.

The only way to keep my priorities in alignment is to strengthen my spirit. This means getting in the Word, praying, and letting go of the things that are pulling me away from God. I recommend you try strengthening your spirit like this too. The more you do, the more you will experience His perfect peace and the easier it will be to say no to your fleshly desires.

I AM

The correct viewpoint of God is that He is the self-sufficient, self-sustaining God who has always existed, who currently exists, and who will always exist. He is a miracle-working God who does not change; His character remains consistent. He created all things, and while He reigns above all and has no equal, He is still a personal God. He knows each one of us by name. He goes to where the broken people are and meets them right where they're at. And He loves them too much to leave them there.

Before we ever chose God, He chose us and adopted those who believe in Jesus into His family. John 1:12 (NIV) says, "To all who did receive him, to those who believed in his name, he gave the right to become children of God," As a daughter of the Most High King, I have unlimited access to God's presence. I can approach Him boldly with confidence, knowing I can talk to Him about anything, anytime, anywhere, and there's no limit to what I can ask Him for. He loves me so much and desires the best for me. I can trust that even if His answer is *no* to my prayer, it is a blessing because He sees the bigger picture and knows what's truly best for me. Trusting in His love and wisdom brings peace and assurance in every situation.

God did not send Jesus to condemn, reject, or pass judgment on us. Jesus came to save us from eternal hell. We were separated from God because of our sin, living in darkness. We needed a Savior to lead us out of darkness and reconcile us back to God. Therefore, God sent His perfect Son to die in our place. Ephesians 1:7 (NIV) says, "In him we have redemption through his blood, the forgiveness of sins, in accordance with the riches of God's grace." By Jesus' blood, we are now forgiven for all of our sins. I picture Jesus on the cross, experiencing excruciating pain, knowing He could have saved Himself at any moment instead of me, yet He stayed. In the midst of the worst pain imaginable, He had me in mind and thought, *She is worth it.*

In that moment, Jesus traded His perfection for my flaws, so I am now blameless and made holy. How can I not lay down my life for someone who would do this for me? How can my heart not want to worship and praise Him? How can I not share the good news to everybody? Accepting Jesus not only as my Savior but also allowing Him to be Lord over my life is like finally opening my eyes after walking around blindfolded. I can finally see my path ahead, and I'm discovering my true identity, knowing who I was created to be. Now, I no longer need to fear what lies ahead because I know who the Author is and He is good. The beauty of God is there is always more to discover.

It's in His presence that the longing in my heart disappeared. For the first time in my life, I had nothing missing. When God looked at me, He didn't see my sin. He didn't see my failures or mistakes. All he sees is Jesus' blood; it's as if I've never sinned. It's not something I can earn by doing good work; I just have to receive it. When I try to earn God's forgiveness, it's like going to pay for my check at a restaurant and discovering that it's already been paid for by my friend. There's nothing I can do because I no longer owe anything. The payment has been paid in full. My past can no longer define me because my history died on the cross with Christ and the new me was born with His resurrection.

Now, I take comfort knowing God is the only One who is actually in control. First Chronicles 29:11–12 (NLT) says, "Yours, O LORD, is the greatness, the power, the glory, the victory, and the majesty. Everything in the heavens and on earth is yours, O LORD, and this is your kingdom. We adore you as the one who is over all things. Wealth and honor come from you alone, for you rule over everything. Power and might are in your hand, and at your discretion people are made great and given strength."

Realizing it is God who gives me everything, not of my own works, brings me freedom from striving to be perfect. I was constantly trying to prove that I deserved to be somewhere. It made me afraid to ask questions because I feared they'd realize I wasn't good enough to be in the position I was in. *What if my questions lead to them firing me?* It made me scared to make a mistake in fear of the same thing. I didn't want to be exposed as not living up to the expectation the person had of me. *What if they regret hiring me? What if I really am not good enough?*

Thank you, Jesus, for the revelation that You place me in the positions and places I find myself in. If God didn't want me there, I wouldn't be there. My stamp of approval is the fact that I *am* there. God tells us to work on everything as if we were working for Him, so as long as I'm stewarding what He gives me well, I will be taken care of. When things seem to take a turn for the worse, I can trust that God has a way of making all things turn out for good and ensuring His plan prevails. He is the One who provides the provision. God makes a way where there is no way. Even the things the enemy sends, God can use for our good. From experience, I can trust God's provision in my life, not only with where He calls me, but also in the midst of uncertainty and hard times.

My Sophomore year of college, my dad got really sick. I came home from college one weekend and didn't realize how bad it had gotten. He couldn't sit at the table and eat with us anymore because it was too painful. He couldn't even lift his own fork. I noticed he would go in our pool in the middle of the night, so I asked him why. He said it was the only thing that gave him temporary relief from the pain. I realized in that moment the pain was never-ending. As my eyes began to water and a lump formed in my throat, I had to hold back my emotions. I had to be strong for him and act like everything was okay. Only the family knew at this time what was going on. I handled him being sick so well...at least that's what everybody thought. I bawled myself to sleep every night, praying and wondering why this was happening.

He's in so much pain, and I can't do anything to help him. I saw him falling into a depression that scared me. My soccer season was coming around soon, and my dad wasn't going to be able to come watch me play. This would only push him further into a depression because he hadn't missed a single game since I was three years old. It brought my parents joy to watch me play. My parents and sister would drive six hours round trip twice a weekend to support me at my games, and then they would rewatch it online after. I worried about how this would affect my dad's mental health being stuck at home while my mom and sister came and watched me play.

Then, COVID-19 spread and the whole world shut down. Let me be clear: the enemy is the one who brought this virus, but God used it for good in my family. I got sent home from college, and my family was able to be together with my dad during this time. His spirits began to rise, and He was getting better. My season got moved from the fall semester to the spring semester. Never in the history of the NCAA have they moved a season, but God makes a way where there seems to be no way. By the time spring semester came around, my dad was well enough to travel again, and he only had to miss limited games. God already did more than I could ever hope for, but He continued to exceed my expectations.

Beyond his health struggles, hospital bills were coming in, business was slow due to covid, and my family was struggling to pay for everything. I felt like I was a burden because my parents were also paying for a part of my tuition that my scholarship didn't cover. Again, nobody knew this except my family. Out of the blue, my coach called me and said he wanted to adjust my scholarship to a full ride effective immediately. God is so good! When I took my hands off of everything and prayed for God to intervene, He supplied everything we needed and more. My life got instantly better in His hands than in my own.

CHAPTER 7

BOUNDARIES

I struggled because I wanted to love my Bible and pray, not just when I needed something or to check off a box, but I just never felt naturally inclined to do so. I wanted to be like the Christians who truly loved their Bible and had a lifestyle of praying. But how did they do it? *Are some people just born that way? Is there something wrong with me because I think reading the Bible is boring?* I was embarrassed to admit it, but after I graduated, I overcame my pride and finally asked how they cultivated their love for Scripture and prayer. They told me it starts with discipline. The more you read God's Word, the more you desire to read it further. The same goes for prayer. It's just like when you start eating healthy. At first, your body craves unhealthy food because that's what it's used to, but after a while of eating healthy, your body will begin to crave the healthy food.

So, I committed to this discipline. Even though I didn't enjoy reading and found the Bible hard to understand and boring, every morning I listened to an audio Bible while following along in my physical Bible. There were times when I even fell asleep listening. Initially, I didn't notice much difference. Some days, I didn't fully grasp what I read. But gradually, I began to feel a change—something better. After a few months, I carried myself differently, with a confidence only God could provide.

I remember my Holy Spirit group leader telling me a year later that I carried myself differently—that my light was shining so brightly now. When I first joined the group, my light was barely flickering, so this affirmation showed me people *were* noticing the transformation I was experiencing internally. It's like going to the gym; you don't see results immediately, but after a few weeks, you start feeling different, better. And eventually, others begin to notice the changes too.

I'm incredibly grateful I persisted with this discipline because now I cherish my Bible, finding it anything but boring. It brings me hope, strength, comfort, and guidance. Most importantly, it reveals who God is. Our future really is determined by the little things we do every day.

Creating clear disciplines ensures you get the results you want instead of just letting life happen to you. A key component of discipline is setting boundaries.

It's good to pre-decide your decisions before you are clouded by feelings. Boundaries may feel uncomfortable at first, but setting them helps us make better decisions—decisions that our future selves will thank us for.

Sometimes it's hard to set boundaries because deep down, we don't feel worthy enough to seek after a big win in an area of life, or we believe we're not as important as others. It can feel like we are being too demanding for having needs, wants, or desires. The truth is, you are not asking too much because you have needs, wants, and desires. Everybody has them. They are important and should be heard and respected. Setting boundaries and sticking to them actually boosts self-esteem. *My time and needs are just as valuable as anyone else's,* and recognizing this has been an empowering step in my personal growth.

The "act as if" tool can be helpful if you struggle with setting boundaries, which means you act like you are already the person you aspire to be. To do this, make clear boundaries for yourself and stick to them no matter what feelings arise. It may feel uncomfortable at first and go against everything you feel you should do, but by sticking to your boundaries, you will ultimately feel better. Every time you stick to your boundary, you are showing yourself respect and reinforcing your self-worth; you communicate to yourself and others that your needs and values are important. I am confident this practice will positively affect your self-esteem, as it did mine.

With my dating life, I made the decision to only accept dates with guys whose beliefs align with mine. If I'm not interested in a guy, I won't entertain him just to have someone to talk to. I'm not interested in wasting their time or mine. If you're going to play games, then I'm not interested. If you're not dating to marry, then I'm not interested. If your actions don't back up your words, then I'm not interested. After three dates, if we don't seem compatible, I am not going to see them anymore. While it's enjoyable to have someone to talk to, feelings complicate things and make it tempting to settle and overlook things I normally wouldn't be okay with. Lastly, I committed to not kissing strangers anymore and maintaining my boundary of saving myself for marriage. These choices have protected my heart and over time elevated my standards immensely. I now recognize my own worth and refuse to settle for anything less than I deserve. Plus, these choices are honoring my future spouse.

When it comes to friends, if you always speak negatively about other people, we can't be friends. Chances are they are probably talking to others about me, and I don't want to participate in the negativity. If I keep falling into bad habits that pull me away from the person I want to be when I'm with you, then we can't be friends. When I'm obeying what God tells me to do and if you can't respect that, then we can't be friends. I trust that God rewards obedience, and if losing friends for following His path is the result, I can rest knowing He will bring the right people into my life.

I believe in the principle of "iron sharpens iron" and seeking relationships that uplift and strengthen me. I am very selective with the voices I allow to speak into my life because I see now they can either push me toward my calling or talk me out of it. I've learned to protect what God has placed in my heart because not everyone has experienced God the way I have. When I share my dreams with the right people, they don't laugh, dismiss me, or tell me it's never going to happen. Instead, they encourage me and believe in those dreams with me because they know the same God I know and they believe in me.

Everybody has the potential to know God personally and live a fulfilled life; however, it's your daily disciplines that make the difference. I have found that to live my best life, I need to take care of my mind, body, and spirit, so I even set boundaries with myself.

Every morning, I have a quiet time with God before I start my day. I read His Word and pray. I cannot look at social media or my emails until I complete my quiet time. While I get ready, I listen to worship music, renewing my mind and spirit. I also do my best to move every day, whether that be a walk or a run. When I neglect my quiet time or skip getting some sort of workout in, I find myself feeling more down during those times.

It's important to be self-aware, knowing what boundaries would help you specifically. Sometimes you'll notice you are more likely to fall into temptation at a specific place, with certain people, or at a specific time. For me, I noticed I kept falling into temptation to text guys I shouldn't be texting when I was drinking. When I would drink, it would make me feel more lonely and I would want attention. These excuses just enabled me to keep doing it. Any other time, I didn't have a problem with it. God told me He wanted me to stop drinking alcohol for all of 2023. I set this boundary for myself, and it helped me tremendously to break that bad habit. I completed the year without ever falling back into that temptation, which made me feel proud of myself.

With my family, I've set a clear boundary: I will follow what I feel God is telling me to do, not just what I think my dad wants. I've already expressed my need for space to discern God's guidance apart from their strong opinions. This decision has helped me become confident in my own beliefs instead of simply conforming to theirs. Now, I trust my own opinions enough and am confident in who I am; I don't morph into what I feel like I *should* be or do.

With anything, I began embracing discomfort as a sign of growth. I set a personal boundary not to allow my ego to get in the way of me growing. If I need help, I will ask. I'm not going to allow the fear of failure keep me from trying anymore.

With my staffing job, at first, I felt the need to be available to my clients every minute of the day because I didn't want them to leave me. They hired our company as a third-party vendor to find qualified candidates, interview them, and present their company with three to five candidates that would be the perfect fit for their team. My clients run corporations, and their time is valuable, and I felt fortunate they chose me. My actions were telling myself they are more important than me or the people I am with because of their title or position. But then I shifted my perspective. I am good at my job, and I ensure they are taken care of in a timely manner. I used to hate when one of my dad's clients would call him during our hour-long drive to soccer practice, yet now I find myself doing the same thing.

I decided I didn't want to do that. I want to be present with the people in my life and not miss moments. I set a boundary for myself: I'm not on call 24/7. If something can wait until tomorrow, I'll address it then. Their needs aren't more important than my personal life, and it's okay to set boundaries with my job. By enforcing this boundary it helps prevent experiencing burnout, I am happier, and on top of that, my clients didn't leave me. Thus proving again that standing up for what you need does not make you too much.

People will take advantage of you if you let them. By making clear boundaries, it helps all parties involved because it establishes clear expectations and again, shows you and everybody else that you deserve respect.

Moreover, it's okay to say no to something and not feel obligated to give a whole explanation. If you struggle with pleasing people, it's easy to fall into the mindset of thinking, *I have to do this* or *They'll be mad at me and won't want to be my friend.* This mindset focuses on earning people's love instead of recognizing that you are enough on your own. If they don't want to be your friend because you are not at their beck and call, then you don't want to be their friend anyway.

I have a friend who loves drawing and is incredibly talented at it. Everyone began requesting her to draw something for them, turning it into a chore rather than a passion. When she felt called by God to create something for someone, she did it effortlessly and with love. However, when she felt obligated to draw for someone, it became difficult and unenjoyable. After discussing it with her, she felt like a bad friend for saying no to people and worried that they wouldn't like her as much.

In reality, she was sacrificing her own happiness and wearing herself out to please others. The right people will love you for who you are, not for what you can offer them, and those are the people you want in your life. People will walk all over you if you let them. Setting boundaries isn't selfish; it's necessary to protect your own happiness and well-being. There's a tangible difference between doing something out of love versus obligation, and God calls us to reflect love. To do that, we need to respect and love ourselves enough to make ourselves a priority and take care of our own needs first. When we do this, we can serve others from an overflow of love.

Overall, establishing and maintaining boundaries in my life has been transformative. I now honor my time and needs without guilt, and I've gained a newfound sense of self-respect and value. I no longer feel like a burden for having basic needs. This journey has taught me that setting boundaries isn't selfish; it's essential for living authentically and with purpose.

CHAPTER 8

STRIPPING OFF COMPARISON

In business school, we took the CliftonStrengths Assessment, a test designed to help you understand your top strengths. My number one strength is competition. While healthy competition can be great, it can also be taken too far and end up holding you back. I made everything a competition, and I didn't compete to have fun...I competed to win. Keenly aware of other people's talents and gifts, my measurement of success was based on how well I did compared to other people. Competition is rooted in comparison, so with competition being so prevalent in my life, comparison is something I've struggled with.

The world pushes comparison on you. My sister and I are only a year apart, and we were compared in everything—school, sports, even our looks. As I got older, I shied away from doing a lot of things because I wasn't sure I would win. Even if there wasn't a technical *winner*, I wouldn't do something if I didn't think I could measure up to the other people doing it.

Comparison was starting to hold me back more and more. It only steals joy and diminishes the unique gifts God has given you. I had to find a way to strip off the need to measure up to other people.

When I got out of college, I started working in sales and recruiting. I was being trained by a few different people. I would shadow them and see how they would handle sales calls and meetings with potential clients. Honestly, I felt so out of my league, but of course, I never said that. As I tried to mimic what they were doing, I didn't have the same effect. I grew frustrated because all of my life people told me I would be good in sales, yet here I was failing at it. So, in comparing myself to the other members on my team, I felt so inadequate. When my boss sold, she was very assertive and direct. They weren't going to push her around. When my coworker sold, she knew the market better than anyone. It didn't make sense not to use her. When I tried to lead with being assertive the client didn't take me seriously—partly because I was 22 years old and they were Executives and partly because that's not my personality. I was just learning the market, so I definitely failed by mimicking my coworkers. I really felt like I didn't belong, but I didn't know where else to go.

One day, while talking to my dad, he told me to quit comparing my rookie self to people who've been doing this for years. Our measurements of success are not the same. This realization gave me freedom because I had been feeling like a failure for not measuring up to the same standard as others, not realizing I was actually doing a great job considering that I was new. By constantly comparing myself to others, I made myself feel like I didn't belong and discounted the wins I had, which I should have been celebrating.

He then advised me to stop trying to do what everybody else is doing and instead focus on what works best for me. He suggested that if I see something someone else is doing that I like, I should add it to my toolbox, but I don't have to adopt everything. Furthermore, he encouraged me to seek advice from those who excel in areas where I struggle. By leaning into my own strengths and humbly seeking help, I began to experience success.

I have a bubbly personality. I've always connected with people by genuinely showing interest in them and finding common ground to bond over. When I aligned my sales approach with these natural strengths and quit comparing myself, I found success.

Not only was I building confidence in talking to strangers regardless of their age, title, gender, or personality type in my job, but to my surprise, I discovered that connecting with others is tied to my purpose. It's actually a gift from God. I may not be able to sing on the worship team, and I may not know how to work in the production booth, but there is a place for me on the connect team at my church, and it's a perfect fit.

First Corinthians 12:14–19 (NKJV) speaks to this: "For in fact the body is not one member but many. If the foot should say, "Because I am not a hand, I am not of the body," is it therefore not of the body? And if the ear should say, "Because I am not an eye, I am not of the body," is it therefore not of the body? If the whole body were an eye, where would be the hearing? If the whole were hearing, where would be the smelling? But now God has set the members, each one of them, in the body just as He pleased. And if they were all one member, where would the body be?"

Each one of us has a unique place in the body of Christ. If we were all the same, essential roles would be missing, hindering the church from thriving. When we get caught up in comparing ourselves, we might try to fill positions that weren't meant for us, leading to frustration instead of fulfillment.

This reminds me of when kids play with a shape-sorting cube to learn their shapes. They are given a variety of block shapes, and the goal is to put each shape in its correct spot. As they learn their shapes, sometimes they mess up and try to force a square to fit into the triangle spot. No matter how hard they try, that square is not going to fit. Not because the square is less than the triangle, but because the square wasn't designed for that area. It's frustrating when you want the square to fit so badly, but it won't. As an adult watching, I want to tell them, "Don't worry! There's a place for that shape," and show them where it is. However, they often want to figure it out on their own. When they are tired of struggling, sometimes they'll ask where it goes. I show them the spot that was designed specifically for the triangle, and it fits in perfectly with ease.

In the same way, I believe God sees us struggling to fit into roles or callings that aren't meant for us. No matter how hard we try to force ourselves into those positions, we end up feeling inadequate and drained. It's exhausting to maintain an image that doesn't reflect who we truly are. God lovingly encourages us to seek Him, knowing exactly where we belong. God wants us to ask Him! He knows exactly where we fit in this world. The calling and purpose He has for us will fit like a glove. There is nobody better suited for the calling on your life than you. We all have a part to play in the body of Christ, and there's a place that only you can fill. It's time to recognize your unique gifts and step into the person God has called you to be.

I had never used this connecting gift to serve God, and when I did, I saw it in a new light. I have a gift for making people feel seen and welcomed when they enter God's house. What an honor and privilege it is. As I began to cultivate this gift to honor God, I became deeply thankful for the boldness He gave me. I pray for God to give me eyes to see His people and the words to speak as I serve each day. Now, I leave church feeling fulfilled. I don't have to be jealous of another person's gift because I've found mine. I truly appreciate the gift God gave me. What an honor it is to have a specific place in the body of Christ, chosen specifically for me. And you have one too; each of us has a unique role to play, crafted by God to make a difference. Embrace your gift and step into the purpose He has set for you.

Another challenge I faced was falling into comparison due to a lack mentality. I grew up not wanting for anything, so it didn't make sense that I had a lack mentality. I realized I spent most of my time with my dad, who, despite now being successful, still carried his poverty mindset from his upbringing while I was growing up and passed it on to me. This mentality had infiltrated into my own thinking, causing me to fear scarcity even though I had never experienced it firsthand. The danger of a poverty mindset is that if left unchecked, it can affect every aspect of your life.

I used to believe that if someone else succeeded, it meant I had somehow lost. This mindset drove me to take control in my dating life, fearing there were only a few good Christian men left, and even they were quickly being taken off the market. Every time I saw someone's engagement announcement, it felt like my chances of finding a partner were slipping away.

Similarly, when I started my sales and recruiting job, I entered a competitive environment where others had spent years building their client bases. I felt discouraged because it seemed like the market was saturated and there were no more clients for me. I thought, *They already have every client; how am I supposed to get any?* I was thinking so small. There are so many markets that have been untapped that I could score big in, but all I saw was there wasn't going to be enough for all of us, so it became a competition.

The truth is, nobody's success is robbing my potential. The Kingdom of God is based on abundance, not scarcity. I can trust that whatever is for me will be for me. I needed to change my mindset from *their win is my loss* to *God is in the room, I must be next.* I identified the root of when this mindset started for me, and I prayed the spirit of poverty off of me in Jesus' name! Then, I found scriptures that declare the Kingdom of God is based on abundance, and I began meditating on them to renew my mind. Whenever the lie crept in that there wasn't enough, I countered it by declaring, "Thank you, Jesus, that You are an abundant God." This helped me align my thoughts with God's truth and trust in His provision in every aspect of my life.

After I worked through the lack mindset, it was easy to celebrate everybody's wins and be genuinely happy for them. With God, there's always more where that came from.

The third challenge I faced was falling into comparison through social media, which often left me feeling discontent with my own life. Seeing peers post about job promotions, engagements, or baby announcements made me feel like I was falling behind schedule. I wanted to be where they were.

God told me I needed to stay in my lane. It's like a relay race in a track meet; if you start veering into someone else's lane, you risk disqualifying yourself. Similarly, when I let my eyes wander to other people's lives, I risk disqualifying myself from what God has for me because I lose sight of my lane—where God's taking me. With God, no season is wasted. He knows how to align the perfect timing, so I can trust whatever is for me will be for me in due time. I can take comfort in knowing I'm on God's calendar, and He is never late. The more I keep my eyes on Jesus, the easier the race I am running becomes, and now I am able to go the distance. What God has for me is worth the wait.

With that being said, one of the hardest things for me to admit to God was my struggle with body image. I was learning to invite Him into the different areas of my life, but this one was off-limits for a while. As I scrolled through social media, I was quiet, but my heart was loud. God sees our hearts, so He already knew, but He was waiting for me to bring it to Him. In my heart, I was comparing myself to what other women's bodies looked like. Thoughts like, *Why can't I look like that?* or *I wish I had her body* often ran through my mind. I would get self-conscious because my stomach didn't look flat like the women flooding my feed. I would ask my sister before posting a bikini picture, "You promise I don't look fat?" The truth is, I wanted validation from other people.

I was surrounded by people who had poor body image, which did not help. I thought the root started in college, but it went back further than that. In high school, I was talking to a guy. I thought we were exclusive, but he ended up cheating on me with two of my closest friends, so I guess we weren't. When I asked him why, he told me, "You all three have something I like. If you had Isabel's flat stomach and Destiny's attitude, then I would have the perfect girl." That hurt, but I moved on so quickly that I never dealt with the rejection. I had to go back and confront the hurt and remind myself that just because he didn't see my worth, doesn't mean I'm not worthy. Furthermore, my body doesn't define my worth either.

While I took a break from social media, I did an experiment. Instead of standing in front of the mirror and pointing out everything I didn't like about myself, I started standing in front of the mirror and reciting affirmations about what God says about me. I would literally hold my list and say each affirmation out loud, going through the list three times. At first, I felt so silly, awkward, and weird, but I stayed committed. Proverbs 18:21 (NKJV) says, "Death and life are in the power of the tongue." By saying these affirmations out loud every day, I'm declaring these things over myself and training my brain to agree with what God says about me, not the enemy. Over time, my thoughts began to shift. I was beginning to see myself the way God does, and the need for man's approval simultaneously decreased. The more I know what God says about me the easier it is to silence a lie.

I still have ups and downs with social media. I've learned to check my heart posture to know when it's time to take a break and refresh my mind with the Word of God. If I feel myself starting to compare, become discontent, or want to post a picture strictly for validation because I feel I'm lacking in an area, then that's my check engine light turning on, indicating it's time to take a break. Back to my affirmations I go, and I spend more time in God's presence. I've found the more connected I am to God, the more content I am with my life.

Later, I realized that whatever you attract people with, you'll feel pressure to maintain. If I attract a guy with my body, I'll constantly be worried about maintaining the same body so he doesn't leave. Additionally, how you present yourself directly correlates with what type of person you attract. I realized I was presenting myself in a way that didn't reflect what I truly wanted. I want to marry someone who is attracted to my spirit and who I am, but I was presenting myself as someone who just likes to have a good time. Having an awareness of how you present yourself will help you attract someone who appreciates you for your true self, beyond just physical appearance or superficial qualities.

Lastly, I fell into comparison with other Christians when I decided to follow Jesus wholeheartedly because I felt like I didn't know enough. It seemed like everybody else was so much further along than me. For a long time, I allowed pride to hold me back from asking questions and learning more about the Bible. Since I had technically been a Christian all my life, I felt I should know more and was embarrassed to ask.

I grew up Catholic, so I wasn't familiar with the prayer lingo. I had a big fear of praying out loud because I didn't sound as eloquent and beautiful as some others did. How do you know what to say? I avoided all eye contact when my community group leader was looking for someone to pray. It made me feel so anxious if I got asked to pray for someone. I had to fight the urge to apologize; it didn't sound like the prayer warriors in the room. I fell back into striving, wanting to do it perfectly.

I researched how to pray and practiced so I wouldn't stutter or sound incompetent next time. I thought my prayers weren't as strong as those who prayed longer or said it in a better way. My research and practice didn't help; I still felt anxious and avoided praying out loud at all costs. I thought, *If only I could pray like my friend or my pastor, then I would always volunteer to pray.*

One day, I was faced with a hard question: when I pray, am I performing for people, or am I communicating with God for Him to intervene here on earth? This was so convicting. I realized I was more focused on what people thought about me than on the actual prayer. There was pride in my heart, and I needed to repent for it and shift my focus.

It doesn't matter if I stutter; I am not praying to perform for people, I am praying to God. God loves hearing my voice no matter how well-spoken I sound. Again, I needed to quit allowing comparison to place limits on myself that I was never supposed to have.

So, I began declaring and reminding myself that the same power that raised Jesus from the dead lives inside of me. I am a prayer warrior because Jesus has given me power and authority over the enemy. Since I refused to let the enemy keep me from using my authority, I forced myself to be in spaces where I had to pray out loud. When the voice in my head would tell me my prayers were inadequate or that I had the worst prayer in the room, I would silence those lies and declare that it's not about me saying the perfect thing. It's not about how long I can pray; even Jesus prayed short prayers.

It's about being a willing vessel for God to use and believing He can do it. There is no pressure on me because my job is just to pray, and it's God's job to handle the outcome. We have to silence the lie that tells us our prayer wasn't good enough, so that's why we didn't get what we were praying for. That's not true. Remember, God is in charge of the outcome, not us. The Bible tells us to keep praying and believing, so just because it hasn't come instantaneously doesn't mean it's not on its way.

I've found that the best way to pray is to follow the ACTS method: Adoration, Confession, Thanksgiving, and

Supplication. First, acknowledge who God is and praise Him (Adoration). Then, confess your sins and ask for forgiveness (Confession). Next, thank Him for His goodness and blessings (Thanksgiving). Finally, present your requests and needs to Him (Supplication). This approach helps to structure your prayer in a way that honors God and aligns your heart with His will.

Overall, I discovered the key to breaking off comparison is to know who I am in Christ. The more I am secure in who I am, the more I have no reason to compete, compare, or be jealous of others anymore. When I find myself starting to get jealous of someone, I compliment them instead or pray a blessing for them so the jealousy can't take root. This way, I turn negative feelings into positive actions, aligning my heart with God's love. The more I read God's Word, the more I see God uses imperfect people like me and the more I see why He created me. I found myself meditating on Psalm 139 often when I was struggling with insecurities, trying to figure out who I am and where I belong in this world.

Psalm 139:13–18

For you formed my inward parts;
you knitted me together in my mother's womb.
I praise you, for I am fearfully and wonderfully made.
Wonderful are your works;
my soul knows it very well. My frame was not hidden
*   from you,*

when I was being made in secret,
intricately woven in the depths of the earth.
Your eyes saw my unformed substance;
in your book were written, every one of them,
the days that were formed for me,
when as yet there was none of them.
How precious to me are your thoughts, O God!
How vast is the sum of them!
If I would count them, they are more than the sand.

These verses make me emotional. I picture God looking out into His creation and realizing there is a need on this earth. So, He begins to form every part of me so intentionally by hand to fill the need. He is all knowing, so not one detail was unthought of or by mistake. He took His time on me, making sure every part of who I am was on purpose for a purpose. The way I look, the way I laugh, my personality, my gifts, my talents, my quirks, and my abilities, everything was on purpose. He designed me with my calling on this earth in mind. There is no one else like me. I am the perfect person for the things that God calls me to. When He was done forming me, He looked at me and was pleased. There is no reason to compare or be jealous of others. He calls me His masterpiece.

How precious are His thoughts about me! Just imagine walking on a beach and seeing all the sand, trying to count the grains in sight and finding it impossible. It's hard to fathom that God thinks even more pure thoughts about us than the number of grains. I realized God is not keeping a record of all my wrongs and replaying them like I have been doing. Instead, He's thinking only good thoughts about me, just as He is about you. It's time to quit comparing yourself and lean into the unique gifts God has blessed you with.

CHAPTER 9

DISMANTLING LIMITING BELIEFS

God says I am the right girl, in the right place, at the right time. I know this is true, but I still struggle to truly believe it when push comes to shove. There's a mindset holding me back.

When doors begin to open for me, my initial response is excitement. Then, when I have time to sit and think about it, I start to wonder, *Why me?* I begin to backtrack…my mind filling with all the reasons why I am not the best choice. It seems too big for me, and I feel I'm not ready. The list of people who are more qualified than I am floods my thoughts next. This is a form of limiting belief that, left unchecked, would restrict me from reaching my full potential.

I remember being asked to lead the salvation prayer at an outreach ministry we were doing at an apartment complex. My immediate response was to suggest someone else who I thought would be a better choice as my mind filled with all the reasons I wouldn't be suitable. *You are going to fail. You don't have the right words to say.*

God convicted me, saying, "I chose you. Why do you disqualify yourself?" The truth is, I still had a limiting belief to work through. I had never done it before, so I didn't feel qualified and didn't want to mess up something that important. I still saw myself as the one who didn't know enough. *Who am I to get up in front of these people and lead them in prayer?*

I was reminded again that God is the One who opens doors, and if He opens a door for me, He will equip me for whatever He's calling me to do. I apologized to God for agreeing with the lies of the enemy instead of stepping out in faith into what He was calling me to do. *God, I won't allow fear to make me turn down another opportunity. If You tell me to do it, then I'll do it, even if I'm afraid.*

Months later, I received another opportunity to speak. My best friends from college asked me to officiate their wedding. I was so shocked, yet honored, that they would ask me. I said yes, but I really couldn't believe they had chosen me. In the following weeks, the enemy bombarded me with all the reasons I wasn't qualified: *You don't know how to create a wedding script. You can't speak in front of all those people. This is the most important day of their lives, and they'll resent you for screwing it up.* These negative thoughts kept coming, and I was close to calling my friends to tell them I couldn't do it.

I prayed and asked God to make it clear if this was something He wanted me to do. *I don't want to do it if You're not with me.* God gave me peace about it, and then one of my classmates from One College confirmed my decision. She said, "I feel like God wants me to tell you that the enemy is trying to steal your voice, but he can't have it." When I was focusing on my own abilities, I felt all the pressure to be perfect. When I considered who I was, I didn't feel like I deserved this honor. In my own strength, I knew I couldn't officiate this wedding the way it deserved, but with the power of the Holy Spirit flowing through me, there's nothing I can't do. It's not about how great I can communicate or write a script; it's about being obedient and trusting that God equips me where He calls me. He is the One who gives the anointing, authority, and approval. When you rest in this truth, God will give you a confidence only He can give.

I've spoken before on my own merit in front of an audience at Sam Houston. There was so much pressure on me to perform well. I was anxious leading up to my speech, during my speech, and after. I got off the stage and immediately wanted everybody's approval. I told God I never wanted to speak again unless His anointing was on me. This time, at the wedding, I felt the Holy Spirit every step of the way. The peace I felt walking down the aisle, while I was speaking, and afterward surpassed all understanding. I wasn't seeking the audience's approval; I already knew I was approved of, and I was on assignment from God. I experienced firsthand that by myself, I am limited, but with God the limits come off.

I love how the apostle Paul says it in Ephesians 3:8 (AMP): "To me, [though I am] the very least of all the saints (God's people), this grace [which is undeserved] was graciously given, to proclaim to the Gentiles the good news of the incomprehensible riches of Christ [that spiritual wealth which no one can fully understand]." Paul is saying that out of every believer in Christ, he considers himself the least qualified to be used by God. However, because of God's goodness and grace, Paul had a huge calling on his life. God used him to preach to the Gentiles and to write most of the Bible's New Testament. Paul knew his limitations and acknowledged them; however, he knew that if God called him to it, He would equip him for it. It's not about how great Paul was, but how great God is.

This holds true for all of God's children. God is the One who empowers us to fulfill the call on our lives. When we maintain this heart posture, limitations no longer matter because nothing is impossible for God to accomplish through us when we surrender to His plan and give Him our obedience.

Our obedience not only affects us, but those around us. At this wedding, I had the honor of standing up in front of people who used to see me drunk at the bar. Now, they saw me as a representative of Christ. Everybody praised me for the ceremony and told me there was something different about it. It's because the power of God was behind every word I was saying and You could feel His presence. Again, it wasn't because I am great, it's because God is. The way God transformed my life was on display, and it opened the door for conversations with me regarding their own faith. One friend asked me, "How are you so joyful all the time now?" I was able to share that it's because I start my day with God every morning. Another person told me they were considering going to church again. When you say yes to God, you unlock a breakthrough—not only for yourself, but also for the people around you.

As I worked through these limiting beliefs, I realized they often stem from the labels we accept or assign to ourselves. Labels can be just as restrictive as limiting beliefs, shaping how we view ourselves and our abilities. In today's culture, it's so common for people to say, "I have anxiety," or "I have depression; I've always had it and I always will." This is labeling yourself and accepting it as your identity. These are real struggles, yes, and I'm not discounting that, but it's not *who* you are. You are a conqueror in Christ Jesus, and these struggles don't have to control your life. We serve a God who is the name above every name and can heal these parts of us. It's time to come out of agreement with what the enemy says and into agreement with what God says. Start declaring that instead of anxiety, you have peace that surpasses all understanding. Instead of depression, thank

God that you have an abundance of joy. Refuse to let the enemy keep you from the good things God has in store for you.

If you need to, seek help to overcome these struggles. True strength is admitting you need help. It's okay not to be okay. We were never meant to do life alone, and the Bible says that where two or three are gathered, there God is in our midst. I'm glad I sought help because my counselor helped me identify a few labels I accepted over the years that I realized were not true or were misidentified.

My main limiting belief was *I'm not good enough.* This label reinforced my limiting beliefs and held me back in many areas of life. I had to revisit my childhood to identify the root of when this belief originated and speak truth into that memory. Then, I invited God in to heal my heart. This lie often tries to resurface in my life. When it does, I meditate on what God says about me and remind myself that I am already accepted and loved. Everything you need for the calling and purpose of your life is already on the inside of you. You lack nothing. Pray for God to prepare you for every dream He has placed in your heart, and know that He is. Quit letting others' opinions of you or your own self-doubt keep you small when you are destined for great things.

Another label I accepted was *I'm not creative.* My mom and sister are both very creative—great at designing and seeing a room and visualizing exactly what needs to be there. This is not a strength of mine, so I always just thought

I wasn't creative. I would shy away from any project that required a "creative" individual. As an adult, I realized I actually am creative, just not in the same way they are. When I took myself out of this box, I saw I had a special gift I had been killing by comparing it to theirs.

I also accepted *I have thick skin*, which my dad often told me when I was young. He was my hero, and I wanted to please him so badly that whatever he said, I unknowingly morphed into. I thought that because I had thick skin, I couldn't show that anything affected me, so I pushed my emotions down and never dealt with them. Having thick skin isn't a bad thing, but the extreme I took it to—always having to be okay—is what made it problematic.

As I've allowed my walls to come down, I've discovered that this label is not the truth. I'm actually quite sensitive. I had to learn how to validate my feelings without letting them rule me. Recognizing and challenging these labels has been important in overcoming my limiting beliefs and stepping into my true identity.

Other labels I accepted were simply misidentified. Growing up, I got called bossy. I hated it, so I tried not to be. I accepted the *bossy* label as if it were true. When I got older, my counselor told me, "I can see you are a natural leader," and when I was younger, it was mislabeled as bossy. It prohibited me from stepping up as much as I could because, in the back of my mind, I didn't want to be the "bossy one" who takes over everything. I thought this part of me was bad, but really it's a great quality to have when stewarded correctly.

Another label I accepted was *I am a perfectionist*. Did God make me a perfectionist, or did He give me a gift for having attention to detail? The way God created me with a gift for attention to detail is valuable, but I was never supposed to carry the pressure to be perfect. Simply redefining these labels has made me more confident in who I am.

You need to know that God didn't make a mistake when creating you. Any labels you've accepted that don't align with what God says about you need to be stripped away. Ask God to help you see yourself as He does. There is a reason you are the way you are; it's time to start seeing your personality in a positive light as it was intended to be. It's time to step outside the box of limitations you were never meant to have and embrace your true potential. God has big things in store for you. Step out of the box, stop disqualifying yourself, and embrace the possibilities.

CHAPTER 10

COMING OUT OF HIDING

"Ashley, where did you put your picture that was on the fridge this time?" my mom would ask, knowing I'd hidden it again.

"Some place you won't find it this time," I'd reply.

The picture in question was from when I had just gotten braces. Honestly, I wished I could erase any picture of me from the time my permanent teeth came in to the time I got my braces off. My teeth were very messed up, and I was frequently reminded of this by others. *I was made fun of enough as a kid; I don't need to hear it now.*

Unfortunately, not everybody shared my opinion. My dad got a mug with pictures of my sister, my brother, and I from that time period. He used it all the time, and I hated it. I thought about "accidentally" dropping it on the ground. My stomach was in knots every time any picture was shown from this time period, and my dad's favorite mug was a constant reminder.

I remember being at a friend's house when I was ten and her four-year-old cousin was over. She asked me why my teeth looked the way they did. Embarrassed and ashamed, I tried to keep my mouth shut the rest of the time so she didn't ask that question again in front of my friend.

These remarks happened on the soccer field too. It was their favorite way to trash talk. Whenever I beat them, they'd say, "At least my teeth don't look like yours." Thankfully, most of the time no one else heard it, which was a small relief. I already knew I wasn't the pretty one, but I didn't want anyone to know that others made fun of me for it.

Sadly, there is one distinct memory I have of when one of my teammates heard the comment. At halftime, she ran to tell the coach, who happened to be my dad. I felt so humiliated. I always tried to move past the comments quickly to avoid drawing more attention to myself. These remarks always made me want to disappear. I often wondered how embarrassing it must have been for my dad, having one of his players run up and tell him something humiliating about his daughter in front of the whole team. Part of me wanted to apologize to him for looking the way I did, and part of me wanted to run away crying. Instead, I took a deep breath and pretended it didn't phase me. If I acted like it wasn't a big deal, maybe I could convince everyone else of it too.

I learned young to build up walls to protect myself and deflect. I got really good at changing the subject quickly. "Well, I got an A on my exam," or "Did you like my assist in the game?" In my mind, I had to prove to myself and others that I brought value in other ways by succeeding in everything else.

When I got my braces off, those comments stopped, and I did everything in my power to hide any memory of that era. I went from being made fun of for having "Sponge Bob's teeth" to being on homecoming court. It felt like one extreme to the next, and I didn't want to go back to how people used to view me. An irrational fear haunted me: if people saw my old pictures, they would all of a sudden revert to seeing me like that—not good enough. It doesn't make logical sense today, but subconsciously I believed it.

One summer when I was home from college, Tyler made a comment about an old picture of me that I had forgotten was on the wall. The comment wasn't even bad, but it triggered something inside of me. I immediately took the picture down and shut down emotionally. I didn't want to talk to him. I felt deeply betrayed and couldn't understand why. His comment didn't warrant such a strong reaction from me, so I knew I needed to sit with this emotion and uncover the root of my hurt.

I journaled about what I was feeling to God and uncovered that he had triggered something deeper—an accumulation of all the undealt-with pain from being teased growing up. Inside, it felt like a personal attack on me, like he couldn't love all of me.

After I graduated from Sam Houston, I was voted "Best Smile" at One College, and I was genuinely shocked. When I told my parents, they weren't surprised at all. They said I had a beautiful smile. Nobody was shocked but me. It's hard to explain, because while I could see that I had a nice smile, there was a disconnect between what I saw and what I believed deep down. *Other people voted for me?* I couldn't believe it. That's when I discovered I still had another layer to peel back. I realized I was the one who didn't fully love myself. No matter how many compliments I received, they didn't address the root of my insecurity, which continued to linger and affect my self-perception.

I was ten years old. Who deserves to be treated like that? No one. My counselor encouraged me to write a letter to my ten-year-old self and tell her what I needed to hear back then.

To my ten-year-old self,

I just want to hug you and never let go. I want to wipe away your tears and tell you it's going to be okay. Their words do not define you. You are a blessing, not an embarrassment. I wish you could see the sparkle in Dad's eye when he talks about his little girl. If only you knew that out of every kid in the world, Mom and Dad still would have chosen you. You are so loved. I wish you could see the joy you bring everyone and the way you light up a room. You are too valuable to have ever been hidden. Most importantly, you need to know God didn't make a mistake creating you, and He loves you just the way you are. You were enough then, and you are enough now.

By going back, healing, and affirming the ten-year-old me, I have eliminated the impact this past pain has on my life today. Now, I am so sorry I ever felt ashamed about her, and I have no reason to hide her. This helped give me freedom from needing to look "perfect." It's really never been about how perfect I can look. I've always been worthy simply because I am His.

I began to see that the memories I've kept hidden are the ones I'm ashamed of. During my three wild years in college, I was adamant that my friends not tell my parents about any of the guys I talked to or kissed. Now, I see it's because I wasn't proud of what I was doing. I was hiding it because I felt ashamed and knew it wasn't the person I truly was.

I did the same with God. I invited Him into my struggles in soccer, and He saved me. But in other areas of my life, I kept Him out because of the shame. God is a gentleman; He won't barge into any area of your life uninvited.

When I graduated from college, I believed that what happened in college would stay in college. However, I realized this isn't true. Eventually, the issues you ignore will catch up with you, and you'll have to deal with them. For example, my unresolved feelings about being made fun of while growing up continued to affect me as an adult, and I didn't even realize it. Until you confront and address your pain, it will continue to impact your life and how you view yourself today. It's difficult to relive those memories, but confronting your hurt can lead to healing and bring more freedom to your life than you might have thought possible.

Although I was healing, I still had the challenge of overcoming feelings of being an imposter. Despite dedicating myself to the Lord for several years and seeing positive changes in myself, I couldn't shake the belief that I might be perceived as a fraud if others knew everything about my past. Being confident that I've had a lot of personal growth and my life has been transformed by God hasn't erased moments of still feeling like somehow I am pretending, especially when I remember how different I lived a few years ago.

Satan enjoys showing me a rear-view mirror filled with my sins and failures, trying to convince me I'm not good enough for God to use. He attempts to instill a limiting belief that your past disqualifies you from fulfilling God's calling. I kept thinking there was going to come a day when something from my past would be revealed and it would be the thing that was too much to forgive. I didn't realize I was still carrying the shame from my past choices. Still carrying the embarrassment, I didn't want anyone to know. I often have to remind myself that God knows everything I've done and will do, and He says I am forgiven. This is true for you too: I don't know everything you've done, but God does, and He still says you are forgiven—period.

Another of Satan's goals is to make you believe that you haven't done enough to be worthy of God using you. Galatians 2:16 (NIV) says, "Know that a person is not justified by the works of the law, but by faith in Jesus Christ. So we, too, have put our faith in Christ Jesus that we may be justified by faith in Christ and not by the works of the law, because by the works of the law no one will be justified." The Apostle Paul assures us that our right standing with God is not based on our own efforts, but solely on the blood of Jesus. Therefore, you are not pretending or wearing dress-up clothes; the transformation in your heart when you accepted Jesus was real. You've been made new; this is the real you. You are the real deal, and God wants to use you right now.

The enemy will try and convince you that you're the only one who struggles with something, so you should keep it hidden or else people will judge you. This tactic is to keep you stuck in shame so you won't step out into all God has for you. The Bible says in James 5:16 (NIV), "Therefore confess your sins to each other and pray for each other so that you may be healed. The prayer of a righteous person is powerful and effective." There is freedom and healing in telling someone about your sin, but it's important to tell the correct people. Share with people who walk with the Lord and are a safe space that you can trust.

God blessed me with an amazing godly community. They encourage me and help call out my God identity. Having these friendships is such a gift. They celebrate with me when something good happens in my life and sit and pray with me through the bad times. I love doing life with them. They push me to be better every single day and call me higher when I'm falling back into old habits. When I have temptations, they remind me of the God call on my life.

I remember God told me to tell them my secret—one I promised I'd take to my grave. I told Him, "Absolutely not!" The next day, we met around a table to have a meeting about our podcast, Eden Awaits, and I started to feel my chest tighten up. I went to the bathroom and wrestled with God. I knew what I was feeling would go away when I told the girls, but I didn't want to tell them. "God, they are going to think differently of me. They are going to think I am the nastiest person in the world. They are not going to want to be my friend anymore. I've lied about this so many times in my life, why tell the truth now?" God told me so clearly, "Because the truth will set you free."

I gathered myself and walked back to the table. The other three girls are just laughing and having a great time, not knowing I am over here struggling to breathe. Finally, I interrupted whoever was talking and said, "I'm sorry I have something to tell y'all and if I don't say it now, I'll chicken out." I had their undivided attention. I opened my mouth and no words came out. I just started crying. I realized I've never said this out loud before and I couldn't get the words out. In the midst of me crying, I told them my deepest darkest secret. I used to struggle with pornography in high school and a few times in college.

The weight on my chest immediately lifted after I spoke these words and my breathing returned to normal. Their reaction healed my heart in more ways than I can put into words. First, they honored me for telling them. Then, they told me how much they loved me and that this doesn't make them see me any different. It actually makes them think even more of me for going through struggles and overcoming them. Lastly, they told me I wasn't alone. They each shared a part of their testimony where they had their own struggles. In these moments, I learned it is better to be fully known and free from shame than keep the parts of me I'm not proud of hidden. Their reaction helped give me freedom from something I didn't realize was holding me back.

Again, it's another example of the enemy making you feel like you are the only one to struggle with something and that you are the worst person ever. The enemy wanted me to keep it hidden because he knew once I finally told the people I feel safe with, I'd be set free from the shame. I am so grateful for the safe place and friendships God has cultivated in my life.

When the enemy comes and accuses you of something from your past, you tell him, "No, that's already been paid for!" Satan's accusation has no merit and no grounds for the attack. You are not those things. You are a new creation. You are accepted. You are forgiven. You are loved.

I knew this was the truth in my mind; however, there was still another layer keeping me captive, causing me to believing I disqualified myself from having God's best in my life with a spouse. My counselor asked me, "Why do you have such a hard time believing God has somebody great for you?" The truth is, I feared I wouldn't be good enough for the godly man I've been praying for.

God told me to study Proverbs 31, known particularly for its description of the "virtuous woman." The Proverbs 31 woman seemed unattainable for me. *She sounds perfect, yet I know I'm flawed. I want to be a Proverbs 31 woman, but I've already fallen short.* I've pondered these statements and feelings, and I realized my fear is that the man I am praying for *won't* choose me. I'll tell him some part of my story, and he will be like, "Yikes. Never mind!" God revealed to me that a part of me still views myself through the lens of shame from my past, and this reduces my value in my own eyes. Ruth's testimony in the Bible was the key to opening my eyes to the truth and setting me free.

Ruth was a Moabite widow. Moabite women had a bad reputation, known for promiscuity, bondage, compromise, and idol worship. In Bethlehem, Israelite men did not want to marry a woman with that identity. Although she knew this meant she'd most likely never remarry or have kids, Ruth chose to proclaim her loyalty to her mother-in-law, Naomi, and her God and move to Naomi's hometown, Bethlehem, leaving everything behind. Ruth is about to discover what she left behind cannot compare to what she is going to gain by trusting in God. God defies the odds, and Ruth's identity and reputation were going to be completely redeemed. Behind the scenes, God was working every single detail out!

Ruth happened to glean for grain in the exact field her future husband owned. Later, he said in Ruth 3:11 (NKJV), "And now, my daughter, do not fear. I will do for you all that you request, for all the people of my town know that you are a virtuous woman." This proves her old identity had been entirely shed. Ruth's obedience and faithfulness throughout the story revealed her true character, altering how people perceived her and transformed her reputation. They no longer saw her through the lens of her past; they recognized her as the woman she is—a virtuous woman. She not only got remarried, but she married a great, God-fearing man. Her "baggage" did not keep her from who God ordained for her.

This testimony brought me freedom: my past doesn't establish my worth or disqualify me from what God has for me, nor does it reflect who I am. I, too, have pledged my loyalty to God and have left my old lifestyle behind. So, like Ruth, it's time to stop limiting myself and be confident that God has redeemed me and know that I reflect Him and nothing else. I can be confident that not only am I redeemed, but my obedience and faithfulness to the Lord has also changed how people perceive me. Previously, I did not possess the characteristics of a virtuous woman, but now I do, and others recognize it. I can rest, knowing I will be the right girl for the godly man I am praying for—the man God ordained for me.

The blood of Jesus is sufficient for God to forgive us, so it must be sufficient for us too. Quit constantly apologizing for your past; there is no reason to be ashamed of it anymore because Jesus' blood has washed it away. It was time I forgave myself, and I pray you will forgive yourself too. You may not be proud of all the decisions you've made; nobody is! But the decisions don't define who you are at the core. It's time to let it go and embrace your new identity in Christ Jesus.

Ephesians 4:22–24 (AMPC) says, "Strip yourselves of your former nature [put off and discard your old unrenewed self] which characterized your previous manner of life and becomes corrupt through lusts and desires that spring from delusion; and be constantly renewed in the spirit of your mind [having a fresh mental and spiritual attitude], and put on the new nature (the regenerate self) created in God's image, [Godlike] in true righteousness and holiness."

When something from my past comes up, I can confidently say, "That was the old Ashley. The new Ashley's slate has been wiped clean. The new Ashley reflects Christ. The new Ashley is who God has called for such a time as this." It was time for my mind to catch up to the truth, and the same is true for you. Don't let shame or past mistakes hold you back. Stand tall in the freedom and purpose you were created for. You are destined for great things.

CHAPTER 11

I AM THE RIGHT GIRL

When I took the limits off of God and asked for an awareness of His presence in everything, He began speaking to me through all things—even movies.

I was watching the movie *Alice and Wonderland*, and God began speaking to me about my identity. I realized that I had always been the right person for the opportunities and people God has placed in my life. God was waiting for me to recognize this within myself so I can fully embrace my destined greatness.

In the movie, Alice chases after a rabbit and falls down a hole into another reality—Wonderland. A caterpillar asks her, "Who are you?" Looking confused, she responds, "Alice." The caterpillar replies, "This is the wrong Alice." Alice was predestined to be a champion and defeat the Jabberwocky, but she wasn't sure if she was the right "Alice" for the prophecy. Throughout her journey, Alice begins to remember who she is and recognizes that she is, indeed, the right Alice and has been all along. She fulfills the prophecy by building her faith and naming six impossible things she sees.

In the same way, when I accepted Jesus as my Lord and Savior, I began to live in a new reality. Where things were once impossible, now they are possible with Jesus. In my mind, I identified with the old me: *Ashley, the sinner. Ashley, who is not good enough.* When God opened doors for me, I thought I must be the wrong person. I knew God could do the impossible, and I believed God would do big things in other people's lives, but I had a hard time believing He would for someone so imperfect like me. Yet, I, too, am predestined for big things in this world. It doesn't matter if everybody else can see it in me if I can't see it in myself.

All the compliments in the world won't make me feel good enough because they can't fix an internal problem. It's great to have people around you who recognize your potential and call out the gifts in you, but this can't be your main source of validation. Struggles with self-worth and identity cannot be fixed solely by external praise. Relying on others' validation enslaves you to their opinions, making it easy to follow the crowd, even when they lead you off your true path. You need a deeper, more stable foundation for your self-worth, rooted in who God says you are.

My source of validation and identity needed to come from the One who created me. When my iPhone is dead, it can't serve its purpose. I must plug it into the charger or else it will remain dead. As long as I keep charging my phone, it will be able to function the way it was designed to. The same is true for us. God is our source of life. We can't function in this world the way we are intended if we don't spend time with Him. Just as I recharge my phone every day, I need to recharge my spirit every day by praying and reading the Bible. When I do, I can be empowered to fulfill my purpose. The Bible is alive and powerful. As you read it, it transforms your heart and renews your mind, guiding you where you should go. You can't do the call of God in your life without God.

I've found that when I neglect my time with Jesus, feelings of inadequacy begin to creep back in. I become less confident in the future God has for me, more anxious, and less patient with others. It's dark without Jesus, but the closer I am to Him, the more I experience His peace and joy despite my circumstances.

By reading His Word, I discover the truth, and it's the truth we remember that sets us free. Now that I know the truth, it's my job to enforce the truth, because guess what? No matter how far we are in our faith journey, the enemy will always try to hinder us by placing lies in our minds. It's our responsibility to discard those lies and not accept them.

One time, I was going to my friend's house for a Halloween party. I had only been there once before, and all the houses in her neighborhood looked similar to me. When

I thought I'd arrived at her house, I knocked and a stranger opened the door. I just assumed he was another guest because I could see the party going on in the backyard. As I tried to walk into the house, I asked where the owners of the house were. The man stopped me and asked, "What are you doing?" I proceeded to tell him I was invited by the owner of the house. He said, "I am the owner of the house." I thought he was trying to be funny, so I laughed. Then, his wife walked over and coming to a realization, I said, "I am in the wrong house!" I had to walk to my car mortified by what had just happened. No matter what I said to this guy, he knew for a fact that this was his house and I was not welcome.

Now, I want to ask you this: do you know the truth, or do you just accept anything and believe whatever thought pops into your mind? Second Corinthians 10:5 (NIV) says, "We demolish arguments and every pretension that sets itself up against the knowledge of God, and we take captive every thought to make it obedient to Christ." This means it's our responsibility to test every thought that comes into our mind against the truth, which is God's Word. If it doesn't align with God's Word, then do not accept it. Just as this man knew the truth and told me I wasn't welcome in his house, so we should be with our thoughts. We must confront the lies, evict them, and declare God's Word over them!

For example, what if *I am running out of time for the promise* pops in my head? Rather than letting it stay, I'm going to say, "I don't accept that," and declare Habakkuk 2:3

168

(NLT) over my life: "This vision is for a future time. It describes the end, and it will be fulfilled. If it seems slow in coming, wait patiently, for it will surely take place. It will not be delayed." If the thought *I am not enough* comes to my mind, I'll say, "I do not accept that!" God says I am beautifully and wonderfully made, and I am accepted as His beloved.

Our thoughts are incredibly important because they shape our identity. Proverbs 23:7 (NKJV) says, "For as he thinks in his heart, so is he." It's time to take ownership and ensure that your thoughts align with the truth of who God says you are. Whatever you choose to consume will come out of you. Choose to meditate on what is true. Philippians 4:8–9 (NIV) says, "Finally, brothers and sisters, whatever is true, whatever is noble, whatever is right, whatever is pure, whatever is lovely, whatever is admirable—if anything is excellent or praiseworthy—think about such things. Whatever you have learned or received or heard from me, or seen in me—put it into practice. And the God of peace will be with you."

As I meditated on the truth, the lies of the enemy were exposed and their power over me diminished. After God led me on a journey of stripping away comparison, labels, and limiting beliefs, I discovered that I am the right Ashley— Ashley in Christ. I am exactly the person to fulfill the plans and call on my life. And I always have been; my mind was finally catching up to the truth.

When I became confident in who I am, the need for validation from people or the desire to please them simultaneously decreased. It's not completely gone, and I have to make a choice every day: am I going to please God or people? My heart's desire is to please God. I'm not seeking praise; I'm obeying because God has called me to. I am no longer tied to the world's standards of success, and I am free from the paralyzing pressures of always needing to be the best.

When I step out and follow what I believe God is telling me to do, I no longer measure success or failure by worldly metrics. Instead, I consider it a success regardless of the outcome because I was obedient. I trust that my obedience leads to God's blessings. Even if it seems like a failure, I know there is always a purpose in God's plan, even when I don't fully understand it. I find comfort in knowing that God does not abandon me; if things aren't good yet, He is still at work. I just have to stay the course, ask God what He is teaching me in this season, and be faithful to the last thing He told me to do.

You can trust that your blessings are waiting on the other side of your obedience—not because God owes you for obeying Him, but because He is inherently good and desires to give you good things.

Beyond the blessings God provides, you can rest assured that you are never alone in any circumstance. Even when you have no answers and are unsure of what to do, you don't have to worry. You don't have to rely on your own strength or wisdom.

Once, I got a flat tire and found myself stranded on the side of the road. Personally, I don't know how to change a tire. I could have struggled on the side of the road, worrying about how to figure it out on my own, or I could call my dad. I knew he would fix it easily and get me back on my way. Obviously, I chose to call my dad, and he fixed it. In the same way, we don't have to sit, struggle, and worry about figuring things out on our own. Our Heavenly Father knows exactly what to do and can do it easily if we just call on Him.

Philippians 4:6–7 (NKJV) says, "Do not be anxious about anything, but in every situation, by prayer and petition, with thanksgiving, present your requests to God. And the peace of God, which transcends all understanding, will guard your hearts and your minds in Christ Jesus." When we bring our worries and the things we are going through to Him, we take the pressure off of ourselves to handle it. Instead, we entrust it to the One with all the answers and power, which produces peace, knowing it's taken care of. I don't have to worry about if I am good enough or all the details on how or when He is going to make something happen; I just have to do my part and know He will do His.

There are times when I'm not sure what God is telling me to do. The worst thing I can do is not make a decision because I am so afraid of making the wrong one. God knows my heart and knows that I want to follow His will. Even if I completely miss the mark and make the "wrong choice," no worries. God works all things together for good.

Remember, God is bigger than any mistake you've made (or will make). He is bigger than the labels people placed on you at school. He is bigger than the stock market. He is bigger than any setback. He is bigger than any person. He is bigger than how you grew up. He is bigger than a degree. He is bigger than everything! Quit focusing on what it looks like in the natural world, and focus on Jesus because we live in a new reality. It's not always going to make sense at the moment, but you can trust that whatever God has promised you *will* happen. He is incapable of lying. We have to stay obedient and surrender to His plan for our lives, and we have the assurance it will exceed our hopes and expectations.

Even when the doubts try to creep back in that *I am the wrong girl* or that *I am not good enough,* I'll bring the doubts to God and let Him remind me that He doesn't make mistakes. He reminds me it's not about what I can do, but what He is going to do through me. I'll remember what He's already done in my life in order to build my faith that He'll do it again. I'll trust in His goodness because He is the same yesterday, today, and forever. I'll remind myself that God isn't looking for perfection, so there is no pressure on me. In fact, God uses imperfect people all throughout the Bible to fulfill His purposes.

I never want to miss what God has for my life because I disqualify myself. I want to follow Jesus no matter where He leads and trust that where He calls me, He will equip me. If I stay where I am comfortable, I stop growing and miss out on what God has planned for me. Following Jesus will never be the wrong choice. I know I will only regret allowing fear to hold me back from what God wants to do in my life.

When the dreams God places in my heart seem too big, I remind myself of the seemingly impossible things He has already done. Did God part the Red Sea for the Israelites to escape from bondage? Yes, He did. So, will He make a way for you when He's calling you to do something, even when there seems to be no logical way? Yes, He will. Did Jesus feed over 5,000 people until they were full with just five loaves of bread and two fish? Yes, He did. So, will He provide the provision you need when you step out in obedience? Yes, He will. Did God protect Shadrach, Meshach, and Abednego from burning in the fiery furnace? Yes, He did. So, will He protect you from being broken by the environment you're in when you remain in His will? Yes, He will. This automatically builds your faith that nothing is too hard for God. He just needs your *yes* and He'll do the rest.

It's a daily decision to lay down my life and follow what God wants me to do. It's not always easy at the moment or the most popular, but it is always worth it. You need to know what you believe and why you believe it so you're not easily swayed to follow the crowds. It's hard to go against the crowd if you don't know why you should, and it's even harder when feelings get involved.

It's our job to prepare our heart because whatever we fill ourselves with is what's going to flow out of us, whether that be what we read, watch, or listen to. The best thing you can do is find a quiet space and spend time with Jesus every day. The world is full of noise, constantly pulling you in every direction. God is speaking to you too, but His voice is a whisper. The beauty of a whisper is its intimacy; you have to be close to hear it. Having a personal relationship with Jesus is like constantly discovering new hidden treasure. The closer I get to Him, the more I discover about Him, and the more I know, the more I love. I will never be able to fully grasp the glory of God, but I get to have a lifetime of finding new gems about Him. As I shed the things that no longer serve me, I am able to pick up the treasure God has for me.

The times I neglected making time for Jesus, I had a harder time saying no to temptation because my flesh was weak. Flesh wants to give in to the momentary satisfaction without thinking of the consequences of how I will feel after. By reading the Bible every day, I equip myself with the truth so I won't be easily deceived by the enemy.

When I do fall into temptation, the enemy wants to condemn me and make me feel like I don't deserve grace because *I should know better by now*. The enemy's goal is to get us to run away from God because of what we've done, but God always wants us to run toward Him. I have to remember that I am still human and will fall short, and His mercy still covers me. Although I don't deserve mercy or grace, Jesus gives it to me anyway. God calls us to progress, not perfection. I know I've made progress because my bounce-back time is quicker. I am quicker to repent and not stay in the temptation I felt.

To help me stay accountable, I submitted to a spiritual leader. She is a pastor at my church who I trust immensely. When I choose to submit to a spiritual leader, I am giving her access and authority to speak into my life, whether that be advice, guidance, or correction. I am now accountable to her also, so if I fall into temptation, I make sure to tell her. This is helpful because then we're able to talk through it and keep me headed in the direction I want to go. I also don't have a 360 view of my life, so having someone who can see my blind spots is very beneficial. She gives me wise counsel when I am making a big decision, encourages me, and reminds me of the call on my life during the times I am struggling.

I used to think when I was having temptations, even though I was pursuing God with all my heart, it meant I must not be doing well enough. *I must be backsliding.* The truth is, nobody is exempt from being tempted. Even Jesus, who is perfect, was tempted. It's how you respond to temptation that makes the difference. When I am tempted, I can trust God will always provide a way out. It's during this time I need to seek God more for strength and guidance. If I am really struggling, I also rely on my godly community.

Having a godly community is such a blessing. The lie that I was backsliding was quickly exposed because I have people in my life who remind me of the truth. You need people in your life who you can be completely honest with. Sometimes I'm in a vulnerable spot and I need my friends to pray for me and remind me of what God has said to me. Being around strong women of God has made me a better person, builds my faith, and motivates me to know God more. Your inner circle matters. It's important for their life to be heading in the same direction you want your life to head.

If you're constantly around insecure people, their insecurities can influence how you feel about yourself. Similarly, if you are constantly around negative people, you may start to adopt a negative outlook. Conversely, if you surround yourself with confident people, you'll begin to feel more confident. If you spend time with positive people, you'll start to adopt a more positive attitude.

Surround yourself with people who motivate you to be better through their everyday disciplines. Seek out those who are running alongside you, chasing after the same goals: Jesus and personal growth. Who you choose to surround yourself with will either hinder you from becoming all that God has called you to be or help call it out in you.

If your reflection in the mirror changes depending on who is in the room, it's an indicator that you're not being your true, authentic self. It's time to take off the masks, let

Christ define who you are, and step confidently into the fullness of who God has called you to be. You don't need to change yourself to fit in or please others. Doing so won't fulfill you. There is nothing better than being fully known and loved for who you are. I've shed my layers, and now my reflection remains the same in every mirror, with joy radiating from within. I am fully known and loved, and that's what I was longing for all along.

I don't know the whole plan for my life, and I don't need to anymore because I know the Author. I see the fruits of His love, peace, and joy manifesting in my life every day, affirming that His way really does lead to a fulfilling life. God will open the right doors at the right time. The key is surrendering my plan for His perfect plan. I can trust that with God, I am the right girl, my best days are ahead, and He'll exceed my expectations. I won't have to force anything or manipulate the situation. God will make it happen. What is for Ashley Friedrichs, will be for Ashley Friedrichs. Until then, I am content with where I am because I'm finally living in the freedom Jesus died for, and part of that is knowing who I am.

Now, I ask you this: will you give God a year of your life, fully surrendered, and watch Him do the same in your life? Freedom awaits, so don't waste any more time settling for less than the freedom Jesus died for! The only regret you'll have is not taking this step sooner. The next step is on you; take it now and begin your journey of stepping into the fullness of who God called you to be and embrace all He has for you. He's just waiting on you!

My Prayer for You, Reader

Father God, I pray a blessing over every person reading this book. I declare you will see yourself the way God sees you—that every lie or limiting belief you have believed is being stripped away and you are coming into agreement with who God says you are. You are enough, you are loved, you are chosen, and you are accepted. Father, I pray You are revealing the broken parts of them and healing every wound in their heart. I command any shame to leave in the name of Jesus. Thank you, Jesus, that Your blood covers all our sins. I command any striving to cease in the name of Jesus. God called you by name. You have everything you need in your tool bag. Thank you, Jesus, that we no longer need approval, but are coming from a place of approval. I command that any fear of your future has to cease in the name of Jesus. God has good things in store for you, and they are better than you even think. Thank you, Jesus, for a fresh filling of Your Holy Spirit. Fill them with Your peace, with Your love, and with a boldness to step out into the things that You've called them to, in Jesus' name, amen!

Salvation Prayer

If you've never accepted Jesus as your Lord and Savior and would like to or would like to rededicate your life to Jesus, the Bible says in Romans 10:9 (NIV), "If you declare with your mouth, 'Jesus is Lord,' and believe in your heart that God raised him from the dead, you will be saved."

Pray this prayer: *Father God, forgive me of my sins. Take my sin and by Your grace, I take Your righteousness. I make You the*

Lord of my life. I give You all that I am. I hold nothing back. In Jesus' name, amen.

Give God a Year

Father God, I thank You for pursuing me even when I ran away from You. I'm sorry for choosing other things over You. I don't want to live in this bondage anymore. I want a life filled with joy, love, and peace—a life that has purpose. I want to know where I belong in this world. I want friendships that will build me up and draw me closer to You. I don't want to settle for anything less than Your best for my life.

I want freedom from the weight that's been pulling me down. I want to walk into a room with a confidence only You can give. I'm tired of doing it my way and coming up short. Your Word says You lead to life, so do as You said. I am committed to going all in with You for a year and seeing how it affects my life.

I surrender control over to You. I lay my plans down at the altar and say, "Have Your way, Holy Spirit." Remove the things that can't come with me into my next season. My flesh is weak; I need Your help to walk away from the things that are not good for me. Strengthen me, Holy Spirit. I know You have good things in store for me, but help my unbelief.

Open my eyes to Your truth and help me experience Your love more fully. Thank you for meeting me right where I am, and thank you for loving me too much to leave me there. In Jesus' name, amen!

MEET THE AUTHOR

Ashley is a passionate speaker, prayer warrior, podcast host, and dedicated leader to young adults and youth. With a background in both business and ministry, she blends practical wisdom with deep spiritual insight to inspire and equip others in their faith journey. A former Division 1 soccer player, Ashley carries the heart of an athlete—determined, disciplined, and devoted to the calling God has placed on her life. She finds her greatest joy in walking with the Lord, journaling His whispers, and sharing His truth. When she's not ministering, she loves spending time with family and staying active through sports. Learn more about Ashley and her ministry at ashleyfriedrichs.com.

REFERENCES

[1] "Mental Health Challenges of Young Adults Illuminated in New Report", Harvard Graduate School of Education, https://www.gse.harvard.edu/ideas/news/23/10/mental-health-challenges-young-adults-illuminated-new-report

[2] https://www.thelancet.com/journals/eclinm/article/PIIS2589-5370(18)30060-9/fulltext

Made in the USA
Monee, IL
23 April 2025

16264153R00108